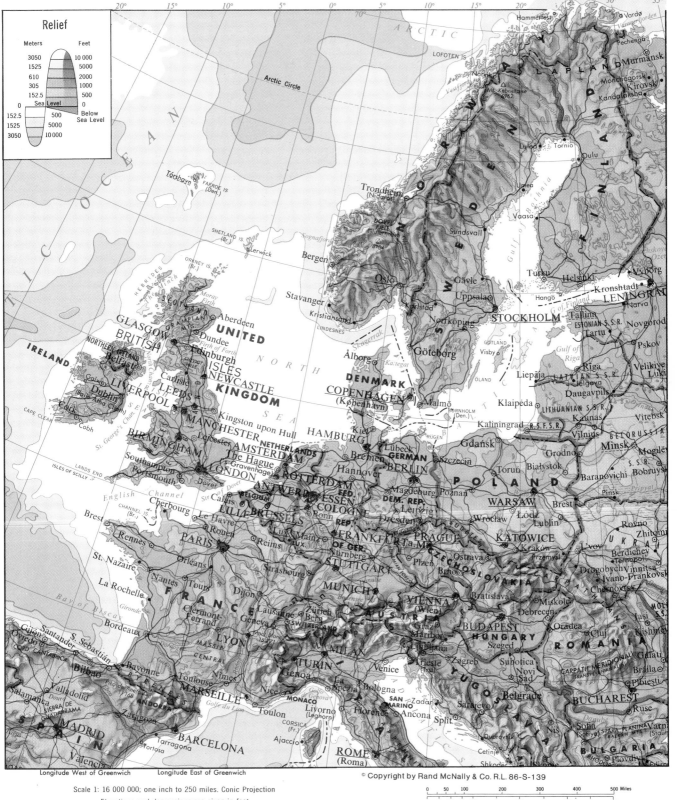

Relief

Meters		Feet
3050		10 000
1525		5000
610		2000
305		1000
152.5		500
0	Sea Level	0
152.5		500
1525		5000
3050		10 000
		Below Sea Level

Longitude West of Greenwich   Longitude East of Greenwich

© Copyright by Rand McNally & Co. R.L. 86-S-139

Scale 1: 16 000 000; one inch to 250 miles. Conic Projection

Elevations and depressions are given in feet

| 0 | 50 | 100 | 200 | 300 | 400 | 500 Miles |

| 0 | 100 | 200 | 400 | 600 | 800 Kilometers |

Enchantment of the World

WALES

By Dorothy B. Sutherland

Consultant: Hereward Senior, Ph.D., Professor of History, McGill University, Montreal, Canada

Consultant for Reading: Robert L. Hillerich, Ph.D., Bowling Green State University, Bowling Green, Ohio

CHILDRENS PRESS ®

CHICAGO

Harlech, on the west coast of Wales

Library of Congress Cataloging-in-Publication Data

Sutherland, Dorothy B.
  Wales.

  (Enchantment of the world)
  Includes index.
  Summary: Explores the geography, history, industry,
arts, and everyday life of Wales.
  1. Wales—Juvenile literature. [1. Wales]
I. Title. II. Series.
DA708.S97 1987   942.9   86-29954
ISBN 0-516-02794-8

Childrens Press, Chicago
Copyright ©1987 by Regensteiner Publishing Enterprises, Inc.
All rights reserved. Published simultaneously in Canada.
Printed in the United States of America.
  2 3 4 5 6 7 8 9 10 R 96 95 94 93 92 91 90 89 88

Picture Acknowledgments
Tom Stack & Associates: © Michael Shisler, 4; © Spencer
Swanger, 32 (right), 86 (top)
Photri: Cover, 5, 8 (left), 14, 18 (2 photos), 19 (left), 20
(2 photos), 21, 23 (2 photos), 24 (left), 25, 28, 30, 31, 33, 34,
36, 39 (2 photos), 41 (right), 43 (left), 51, 52, 54, 58, 64
(bottom), 67 (2 photos), 69 (2 photos), 72 (top right and
bottom), 77, 78, 79, 80, 83, 86 (bottom), 88, 90 (right), 93
(center), 95 (2 photos), 96 (3 photos), 99 (2 photos), 100,
101, 102 (2 photos), 103 (left), 104 (top left), 111 (right),
114
Roloc Color Slides: 6

There is some variety of spelling for names in
Wales. Childrens Press has chosen the spelling
most favored by recent historians and current
guidebooks.

Journalism Services: © 1984 Dave Brown, 8 (right);
© Terence Soames, 75, 84 (bottom); © Ellen H. Przekop, 81,
82 (right)
Nawrocki Stock Photo: © Nadia Mackenzie, 11, 12 (right),
64 (top), 104 (bottom left)
© **M.B. Rosalsky:** 12 (left), 76
© **Joseph A. DiChello, Jr.:** 15
Valan Photos: © 1985 Kennon Cooke, 24 (right), 53 (right),
111 (left); © K. Ghani, 72 (middle right), 74 (left), 91;
© Pierre Mineau, 103 (right)
© **Mary Ann Brockman:** 27, 59, 68, 72 (top left)
Historical Picture Service, Chicago: 32 (left), 41 (left), 45
(2 photos), 48 (2 photos), 50, 53 (left), 61, 62 (2 photos), 63,
71, 110 (left)
© **Bob & Ira Springs:** 43 (right)
British Tourist Association: 74 (right)
© **The Photo Source Ltd.:** 16, 76 (right)
Root Resources: © Betty P. Sorensen, 82 (left)
© **James P. Rowan:** 84 (top)
AP/Wide World Photo: 90 (left), 93 (left and right), 106
(3 photos), 108, 109 (2 photos)
© **Buddy Mays:** 104 (top right, center, and bottom right)
The Bridgeman Art Library: 110 (right)
Len W. Meents: Maps on pages 19, 73
**Courtesy Flag Research Center, Winchester,
Massachusetts 01890:** Flag on back cover
Cover: Farmland in Wales

Gathering shellfish

TABLE OF CONTENTS

This town's name is the longest in the world, but it is simply called Llanfair P.G.

Chapter 1

DRAGON COUNTRY

Llanfairpwllgwyngyllgogerychwyrndrobwllllantysiliogogogoch.

This is a place name, surely the longest in the world. It belongs to a small village in one of the smallest countries in the world: Wales. The language is Welsh, which is also the name of the people who live in that country.

The name translates, roughly, as: Church of St. Mary in the Hollow by the White Aspen near the Rapid Whirlpool and Church of St. Tysilio by the Red Cave. (*Llan*, which occurs twice in that name, means "church." You have just had your first lesson in Welsh.)

If you want to know how to pronounce it, start with a noise like clearing your throat, add an "*l*" sound and get as far as "Chhlanfair" before abandoning the attempt. Knowing that the next to last syllable is always the one stressed in Welsh is not much help in this case.

When the village that bears this long name (please don't expect us to spell it more than once), had a working train station, pranksters kept making off with the sign, although it is hard to imagine how they managed to conceal it. The railway is now abandoned and the station house is a cafe, but you can still see the last of the signs in a museum in Penrhyn Castle near Bangor in North Wales.

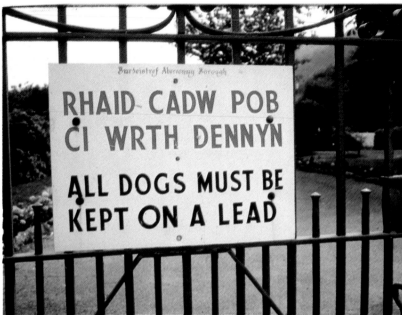

Some bilingual signs in Wales

Wales is attached to the west of England, but do not make the unforgivable mistake of calling it part of England. It is part of the United Kingdom, or Great Britain, which also includes Scotland and Northern Ireland. Wales has its own distinct character and the people are strongly nationalistic. There is an ancient enmity between Wales and England, so if you call a Welsh person English you will not be at all popular.

Any tourist entering Wales from England will at once be aware that this is a very different country. You are entering not just Wales but *Cymru,* the Welsh name for the country. Welsh is a living language and road signs lead to places such as Cwmystwyth. Where have all the vowels gone? (*Y* is often used instead of *i* and *w* is pronounced *oo.* Welsh lesson number two.) Although only about one-fifth of the Welsh people speak the Welsh language (and those that do also speak English), the movement to keep it alive is very strong. In parts of the country—northwest and mid-Wales—ninety percent of the people are bilingual and Welsh is taught from nursery school level to adult evening classes. There are radio broadcasts in Welsh, and an all-Welsh-speaking television station.

Even those who speak only English do so with a unique and very musical accent, which reflects the lilt of the Welsh language. All the people speak English very distinctly—no one in Wales seems to slur words. The visitor does not have to contend with the strangeness of accent that makes it difficult to know what people are saying in other British places such as some parts of Scotland and regions of England.

The Welsh language is Celtic in origin, as are the forms of Gaelic spoken in parts of Scotland and Ireland. Strangely enough, however, Welsh is most closely related not to these languages but to the French (Gaelic) spoken in Brittany. Such are the accidents of history.

On entering Wales, the tourist will see not only strange-looking place names but, on many signs, of all things—bright red dragons! While other countries may have actual creatures like lions, bears, or eagles for emblems, Wales flaunts what to most people is a mythical beast. But the dragon tells quite a lot about Wales, for here history sometimes seems to merge into legend. Here you will be shown the site of King Arthur's Round Table and the birthplace of the famous magician Merlin. Here you will be told tales of sunken villages, lost princesses, and slumbering heroes waiting to rise again.

One legend that even the English have chosen to believe when it suited them is that, in 1170, a Welsh prince, Madog ab Owain, set forth to discover America. Near the little town of Porthmadog is a craggy rock known as Madog's Island from which he is said to have sailed. Also, near the seaside resort of Llandudno, is a flat rock said to be the remnants of an old quay. A plaque there boldly states: "Prince Madog sailed from here to Mobile, Alabama."

Twice the English treated Madog's achievement as historical fact. Once, in the sixteenth century when they were laying claim to land rights in the New World; and once again in the eighteenth century, when disputing with the Spanish over the upper Missouri valley territory. Explorers were produced who claimed to have discovered Indian tribes with Welsh habits of living and Welsh words in their language. It became fashionable for English colonists to claim Welsh descent. Stories of early Welsh presence in the New World were so persistent that some went so far as to say that Montezuma was a Welshman! Once in a while, still, there are those who find traces of Welshness in various North American tribes. Once in a while, on the fringes of a Columbus Day parade in an American city, someone will be seen valiantly carrying a flag for Madog ab Owain.

Wales is full of strange monumental stones and mysterious lakes, not to mention hundreds of ancient castles. The landscape is often swathed in the kind of eerie mist in which it is quite possible to believe in strange happenings and unearthly creatures.

Perhaps the Welsh may be forgiven for embroidering their history with myth and legend for the reality has often been all too harsh. This little country has again and again been invaded and exploited, yet it has preserved its identity. Its ancient tradition of song, poetry, and legend has been very important in achieving this.

Mist-wreathed crags are only one aspect of the Welsh countryside. There are many charming little towns and villages,

*The houses in Pembroke (left) are painted in bright colors while a cottage
in the north (right) gets color from its window box and garden.*

their stone-built houses painted in bright pastel colors. (One gets
the feeling that paint salesmen must do a thriving business in
Wales.) In fact, Wales has a remarkable range of sights to be
seen—in an area smaller than the state of Massachusetts—from
mountain grandeur to farmland, to sweeping seascapes.

In spite of the strange place names, the tourist who comes to
enjoy the sights of Wales will soon feel at ease for the Welsh are
very courteous and quick to offer hospitality, producing pots of
tea within moments of a visitor's crossing the threshold. For the
most part, Wales seems like any other English-speaking country

with people who are very much in step with modern times. The young people are like those in so many parts of the world today — wearing blue jeans, interested in movies and TV, riding motorbikes, listening to rock music. Sometimes, however, the rock music is their own composition and the words are in Welsh. (Mick Jagger is said to have approved, calling the Welsh "real rockers.")

There is no doubt that it is the Welsh language and culture flourishing in it that make Wales a special place. Even the large numbers of Welsh people who do not speak it know in their hearts that it is the persistence of the language that gives the country its soul.

A note on names: you probably know, or have heard of, someone with the first or last name of Lloyd. You can be sure that there is some Welsh strain in the family. The famous architect, Frank Lloyd Wright, for instance, had a Welsh mother and was very proud of this part of his ancestry. He named his own houses, in Wisconsin and Arizona, Taliesin, the name of one of the early Welsh poets. His style of architecture, too, is designed to be a natural merger with the landscape, as the old Welsh buildings were.

There seems to be something of a dearth of last names in Wales. There are so many people called Evans, Morgan, Price, Williams, Thomas, Roberts, Hughes, Jones, Johns. Sometimes people are identified, to avoid confusion, by the place they live: Mr. Price Dyffryn; or by their occupation: Mrs. Johns Grocer. To compensate, there are some imaginative first names: Dylan, Aneurin, Emlyn, Llewellyn. It is said that the novelist Richard Hughes threatened to call his son Mohamet so he would have a unique name in the telephone directory.

Manorbier Castle stands on a cliff top overlooking the sea.

A note on castles: there are some six hundred castles in Wales, more to the square mile than in any other country in Europe. They range from sad, battered ruins, to magnificent turreted piles, to castles built in recent centuries by industrialists to display their wealth.

A note on legends: anyone who is interested only in hard facts will find Wales somewhat frustrating. Everywhere are monuments to myths: stones mark where legendary heroes are said to have been born or to have died and where deeds that possibly never happened are said to have taken place. This is undoubtedly the Celtic heritage at work, for the Celts loved poetry and poetry is not usually concerned with dull reality.

One of the great legends of Wales is about that red dragon that is the national symbol. The story goes that King Vortigen, in the fifth century, ordered a great fortress to be built near the mountain Snowdon. Every day his workmen laid the foundations and after every night these foundations had disappeared. Obviously there was an evil spell at work. The king's wise men told him that the spell could be broken only if the blood of a fatherless child was sprinkled on the site. A seven-year-old boy

14

The red dragon, the national symbol of Wales

called Merlin was found and brought to the king to be slain.

Merlin persuaded the king that he would reveal the real reason the foundations were disappearing. Beneath them, he said, lay two dragons who awoke to fight each night, shaking the earth so that the foundations were destroyed. Workmen dug down deep and, sure enough, found one red dragon and one white one asleep. Merlin told the king that the red dragon represented the Celtic race and the white one, the Saxons. There would always be upheaval in the land as long as the two nations fought one another. The red dragon thus became the symbol of Celtic Wales. Merlin grew up to be the magician who appears in the other great legend of Wales—that of King Arthur and the Knights of the Round Table.

These and other legends appear in the *Mabinogion*, a famous early Welsh book from which Sir Thomas Malory got the material for his fifteenth-century work *Le Morte d'Arthur* and Tennyson his nineteenth-century poems *Idylls of the King*. In our own century, the Arthurian story has been beautifully told by T.H. White in *The Once and Future King*.

Chapter 2

THE FACE OF WALES

"Down yonder green valley, where streamlets meander" is the beginning of the old Welsh song "The Ash Grove." Wales is certainly a land of valleys and streamlets, mountains and waterfalls, lakes, rivers, and seascapes. It is not possible, here, to get too far away from water for the country, which is only 130 miles (209 kilometers) in length, is bordered on three sides by water. (It also rains a lot.)

In the north is the estuary of the river Dee and Liverpool Bay. On the west is the Irish Sea of which Cardigan Bay is a part, the bay that takes a huge bite out of west Wales. In the south is the mouth of the river Severn and the Bristol Channel. The north of Wales is only 90 miles (145 kilometers) wide, the south 100 miles (161 kilometers) wide, and in the very middle Wales is only 40 miles (64 kilometers) wide. The total area of the country is 8,018 square miles (20,768 square kilometers). It has so many scenic beauties that one-fifth of Wales is classified as national park.

The fourth side of Wales borders on England. Here can be seen, in various states of repair, the castles that were built to keep the wild Welsh in their place. Here is the ridgeway known as Offa's Dyke. This was constructed in the eighth century by Anglo-Saxon King Offa of Mercia as a boundary between his kingdom and

The Isle of Anglesey (left) is connected to the mainland by two bridges (right), one for motor vehicles and the other for trains.

Wales and it is still an important symbol of the cultural difference as well as the territorial division between England and Wales.

There is one village on this border, Llanymynech, which fronts on England and backs on Wales. A few hundred yards to the east of it, the official border runs right down the middle of a street. There are people buried in a local churchyard with their heads in Wales and their feet in England. There is an inn with a marker on the bar to show where the border is and, although this is a splendid tourist attraction, the landlord has to pay for it by being liable for both Welsh and English local taxes.

The main regions of Wales are Gwynedd and Clwyd in the north, Powys and Dyfed in the center, and Glamorgan and Gwent in the south. These regions are divided into counties or shires.

NORTH WALES

Gwynedd consists of the island of Anglesey, Caernarfonshire, and Merioneth. Anglesey is separated from the mainland by a

Beddgelert, a mountain village in Snowdonia

stretch of water called the Menai Strait. It is the closest point to
Ireland and has a little satellite island, Holy Island, from which a
ferry runs to and from Dublin. There are two bridges between
Anglesey and the mainland, one for automobile traffic, one for a
railway. On Anglesey you will find the village with That Name
and will be relieved to find that it is now known simply as
Llanfair P.G. And you can pronounce that, right?

The part of Caernarfonshire that juts out into the Irish Sea is
called the Lleyn Peninsula and is dotted around the coast with
charming little villages. Farther east is the magnificent
mountainous region Snowdonia, which takes its name from the
mountain Snowdon—at 3,561 feet (1,085 meters), the highest peak
in the British Isles south of the Scottish border. It is possible to
climb Snowdon on one side by a gently sloping wide path, but as
the path is 5 miles (8 kilometers) long this is no easy stroll. Most
of the mountain is sheer and craggy and can be tackled only by
experienced climbers. Mountaineers come from around the world
to try their skills on Snowdon and it was here that the first

19

The two most famous mountains in Wales, Snowdon (left) and Cader Idris (right)

expedition to conquer Everest trained for the venture. On the ceiling of a hotel in a nearby village you can see the signatures of Sir Edmund Hillary and others of his party who made the historic climb.

In Merioneth, the southern part of Gwynedd, is another of Wales's famous mountains, Cader Idris, which means the chair of Idris. Idris was a legendary giant who was described by some bards as a poet, by others as a warrior. It is said that anyone finding the actual chair and sleeping in it overnight would wake in the morning as either a poet or a madman. Many brave tourists have slept on the mountain to test this theory but none can have hit on just the right spot as all have awakened still sane and unvisited by the poetic muse.

Around Cader Idris lies beautiful scenery much appreciated by the many artists who have come to paint it. There are many lovely lakes (the Welsh word for lake is *llyn*) including the small Llyn Cau that is reputed to be bottomless and to be home to monsters

A section of the ruins of Flint Castle

that rival the one in Scotland's Loch Ness—though that one gets all the publicity. In this region, too, is an area once known as "the California of Wales" or the Dolgelly Gold Belt. Gold from the mines here has traditionally been used to make wedding rings for the British royal family—including the present Princess of Wales.

Clwyd, to the east of Gwynedd, has two shires: Denbigh and Flint. Flint is one of the few industrialized areas left in Wales and the town of Flint, once a prosperous port, is now a factory town. Among its smokestacks can be seen the ruins of Flint Castle, the first of the thirteenth-century castles built by the English king, Edward I.

South of the industrial area lies beautiful mountainous country through which runs a spectacular winding road known as Horseshoe Pass. This winds down to the Vale of Llangollen, which is the setting, each year, for an international festival of music and dance.

CENTRAL WALES

To the south of Clwyd and Gwynedd and bordering on England is the region of Powys, consisting of Montgomery, Radnor, and Brecknock shires. This is the most sparsely populated part of Wales, an area of mountains and moorland, forests and farms, and small isolated villages.

On the eastern border of Montgomery is Plynlimon Mountain, one of a range of five hills. Here rises the Severn, which at 220 miles (354 kilometers), is Britain's longest river. It winds first through a narrow gorge with forests on either side, then through a valley of farmland to leave Wales at the little town of Welshpool. It then flows south through the west of England and back toward Wales at its estuary in the Bristol Channel.

In South Powys—Brecknock and Radnor—lie three little resorts that were famous spas in the nineteenth century when "taking the waters" was all the rage. These are Llandrindod Wells, Builth Wells, and Llanwrtyd Wells. The first of these was first patronized by King Charles II in the seventeenth century and is now a popular conference center. The others are still holiday resorts and Llanwrtyd, situated on the river Ifron, attracts anglers and also climbers and pony trekkers who aim for the nearby Cambrian Mountains. These mountains lie between Cader Idris and the Brecon Beacons in Brecknock. The Beacons, a national park area, are inhabited by sheep and athletic vacationers who want to climb or ride among spectacular views of the surrounding countryside.

Near here, too, are many caves, some that can be explored by adventurous spelunkers (cave explorers), some that can be safely viewed by the public, and some that are known to have been lived in by prehistoric settlers. Other features of this region are a series

Above: The countryside near the Brecon Beacons
Left: A spelunker in a cave in Powys

Lovely, fertile green valleys in Wales are used for agriculture.

of beautiful waterfalls and countless traces of the Roman occupation. Surprisingly, in this unexpected corner of the world, in a little town called Hay-on-Wye, is "the world's largest secondhand bookshop." On the border between south Powys and the English county of Hereford lies a range of hills called the Black Mountains that run into Gwent in south Wales. (Just to confuse things, the Welsh have another hill called Black Mountain in the western region of Dyfed.)

Dyfed is the largest region in Wales, lying in both central and south Wales. Its northernmost shire is Cardigan whose west coast is Cardigan Bay. This part of Wales is not well populated except seasonally by tourists and by students at branches of the University of Wales. Aberystwyth, site of the main campus, leads to yet another marvelously scenic area: the Rheidol Valley.

SOUTH WALES

Pembrokeshire, in southwest Dyfed, has a wild and beautiful coastline, another national park area. It has magnificent cliffs sheltering tiny coves that can be reached only on foot. In the spring and early summer, thousands of wild flowers clinging to the cliffs make this area one huge rock garden.

Wildflowers cover the cliffs on the coastline of Pembrokeshire.

Speaking of flowers, in the small town of Tenby in this region there grows a special variety of daffodil (the Welsh national flower) that grows nowhere else in Europe.

Carmarthenshire, in southeast Dyfed, is an area of moorland and more lovely river valleys, with a small pocket of industry in the east where it borders on Gwent. It is an area containing many traces of the Roman occupation of Wales. At a place called Dolaucothi you can see marks of chisels on rock—the open face of gold mines that were worked by the Romans more than two thousand years ago. Here, too, is one of the first towns the Romans founded in Wales, Carmarthen. Apart from its Roman connection, Carmarthen has an Arthurian connection. Here is located Merlin's Oak. "When Merlin's Oak will tumble down/ Then shall fall Carmarthen town," goes an old rhyme. When a modern roadway was recently built through the town, the oak was carefully removed from its path and transplanted to the

County Museum. Carmarthen was taking no chances. At the site of an old Roman encampment about ten miles (sixteen kilometers) away, is the reputed birthplace of Merlin.

Glamorgan is the region of Wales with the country's only two sizable cities, Cardiff and Swansea. It is an area of great contrast, with much of its natural beauty scarred by industry and the relics of industry. Here is the famous Rhondda Valley where ugly coalmining towns grew up among the lovely hills. (The Welsh author Richard Llewellyn wrote a most affecting novel, *How Green Was My Valley*, about the hard life of the miners and their families, which was made into an Academy Award-winning film in the 1940s and into a Masterpiece Theater production on TV in the 1980s.)

In west Glamorgan jutting out into the Bristol Channel is the scenic Gower Peninsula, sometimes called the Welsh Riviera because of its beautiful beaches. Around its coast are many caves, once lived in by prehistoric settlers and later used by smugglers. These smugglers used to lure ships to be wrecked against the cliffs by showing lights that seemed to promise safe harbor.

Farther round the coast are constantly windswept sands that sometimes shift to reveal traces of prehistoric dwellings. This area of dunes and hollows and swirling sands is sometimes used by filmmakers. For instance, in a movie called the *Seven Graves to Cairo*, the "Sahara Desert" that the actors were struggling through was really this spot in south Wales.

Gwent, in southeast Wales, is separated from the English county of Gloucestershire by the river Wye that flows into the Severn at the town of Chepstowe. Celts and Romans both built fortifications on the high cliff overlooking the river and there the Normans built their first stone castle in Wales. Its ruins still stand in this commanding position.

Unspoiled sand dunes on the Gower Peninsula

Gwent is another area of many Roman remains and among the most fascinating is the huge amphitheater at Caerleon-on-Usk where you can actually sit on the same stone seats that were sat on by gladiators waiting to take part in the fierce fights held in the arena. (This is the arena that some claim is the site of Arthur's Round Table.) Here at Caerwent is one of the first towns ever built in Wales by the Romans and you can see not only large sections of the Roman wall around the town but also some of the foundations of Roman villas.

Everywhere in Wales its history and prehistory are part of the landscape. The mines and quarries—mostly disused; the castles; the Roman remains; the mountains, stones, and boulders; the valleys carved out by ancient glaciers; the countless lakes formed by the melting of the Ice Age—all bear witness to the forces that have shaped this unique country.

Neolithic burial chamber in South Glamorgan

Chapter 3

THE LONG ROAD TO
CYMRU

EARLY SETTLERS

Where did the Welsh come from and how did they eventually
become a distinct people? Little is known about the earliest
inhabitants of Wales, although occasional remains have been
found in various caves. In the early nineteenth century, an
exciting archaeological find of ancient human bones turned up in
a cave in Paviland in Gower. This partial skeleton was christened
The Red Lady of Paviland. However, it later was discovered to be
a man! The fact that all ancient bones have been found in coastal
caves indicates that these early people were hunters without the
tools and skills to penetrate beyond the fringes of the land. Where
they came from, nobody knows.

Wales's long seacoast always made it open to adventurers from
abroad. In Neolithic times, successions of settlers arrived from the
Mediterranean area. These people too, from the archaeological
evidence, seem to have been daunted by the mountainous reaches
and to have kept to the friendlier plains. It was they who first
practised agriculture and introduced the beginnings of trade—as

Neolithic megaliths

traces of an ancient ax factory show. You can still see the remains of a Neolithic settlement of stone huts on the side of a mountain, Yr Eifl, in Gwynedd. The Welsh call it the Town of Giants, granting mythical stature to its old inhabitants; but more common traces of the Neolithic people are to be seen in the remains of great stone megaliths that were family vaults for the important families of the day.

After the Neolithic settlers came the people of the Bronze Age who arrived between 1500 and 500 B.C. They came from central and eastern Europe and were skilled in the use of tools. Apparently they did not know of the plentiful ores that lay buried in Wales and brought their metals from other areas.

Among the peoples who arrived during the Bronze Age were the Celts who came between 1200 and 600 B.C. They brought with them the language on which modern Welsh is based. They were a warlike lot, organized in tribes. The remnants of their culture that

A monument to the Duke of Wellington atop an "iron fort"

endure are the so-called "iron forts," settlements built on commanding headlands and other strong positions from which it would presumably have been easy to drive off marauders. The lack of evidence of battle to be found on these sites suggests that few made any attempt to storm them. Within these forts lived varying sizes of communities and domesticated life was possible. Flocks and herds of animals could be raised and some trade with the world beyond the settlement was conducted by barter. Coins were not yet current.

With the Celts came the Druid religion. In this fierce and mystic cult, rivers and lakes were holy places and Wales was plentifully supplied with these. The main stronghold of the Druids was on the island now known as Anglesey, then called *Mon Mam Cymru,* "The Mother of Wales." When the Romans came, they shortened this to *Mona.* The Romans arrived in Wales around 47 A.D. and reached the Menai Strait in 80 A.D. The Roman historian Tacitus

Left: The Druids exhorting the people not to let the Romans land.
Right: A Druid burial chamber

has recorded what they saw facing them across the water. There they beheld a dreadful horde "pouring out frightful curses with their hands raised to high heaven. . . .At this sight our soldiers were gripped by fear." The Romans were not allowed to retreat, however. They crossed the strait by raft or by swimming their horses over, and slaughtered or captured all the shrieking Druids. They also destroyed the Druids' holy altars and groves.

The Celtic strain has persisted in the Welsh character. The fact that Wales has had few urban settlements has been traced to the old Celtic tendency to spread out into isolated tribal communities. The love of poetry and music, of mysticism and legend, are all traced back to their Celtic heritage.

The ruins of a Roman amphitheater in Caerleon

THE DAYS OF THE ROMANS

The Romans occupied much of Wales for three hundred years but did not conquer all of it. The western promontories, north and south, never fell under Roman influence and many of the remote Celtic enclaves in the mountains seem to have been left alone, probably because it would have been more trouble than it was worth to bring them into submission. The chief opposition the Romans encountered when they first reached Wales came from the leader Caradog, Caractacus to the Romans. He and his followers fought fiercely against the invaders till he was captured and sent to Rome in 51 A.D.

The Romans set up many military camps, built roads, and established two big towns at Cardiff and Caerwent in Gwent. Here many of the Celts settled in, embracing Roman ways of life, adopting the language and system of government.

The great highway the Romans built, connecting north and

*Remains of
the Roman road
near Harlech*

south Wales, still exists in part and, in places, can even be walked on or driven over. Stretches of the modern highway follow its path. This great highway was built not just for troop movement but for transporting lead and gold, for the Romans discovered the mineral wealth of Wales and, with local labor, worked the mines.

This great highway is known as *Sarnau Elen*. There are two theories about this name: some believe it comes from *Sarn y Lleng,* the Causeway of the Legions; some prefer to believe the legend that it means Helen's Causeway. Helen was the Welsh wife of the Roman commander Magnus Maximus. He was acclaimed in Britain as emperor and, when he left for Gaul (France) to set himself up as such, he was accompanied by a Welsh bodyguard. He left the government of Wales in the hands of local people. The Welsh thus claim that they were the first people to whom the Romans ever gave self-government. Maximus, known as Macsen Wledig, is regarded as a hero and many Welsh princes have claimed descent from him.

LEGENDARY TIMES

By the time the Romans left what is now Wales, the native Celts had been infiltrated by an Irish Christian settlement in Pembrokeshire and by Romanized Britons from other parts of Britain. Still more Britons were to arrive after the Romans departed, entrenching the Roman influence more deeply.

The history of the years after the Romans left is far from clear and strewn with legend. It is known that the roads deteriorated, mines were abandoned, internal trade reverted to barter. Venturesome traders who came from Ireland, Gaul, or as far away as the Mediterranean, however, kept some forms of culture and crafts alive.

Christianity, too, came from across the sea. It had a small foothold before—Maximus is said to have been Christian—but it had been the religion of an elite few. In the fifth century, missionaries arrived from Gaul to convert the rest of the people. A missionary center was set up in Glamorgan and a monastery was established in Pembrokeshire by the preacher Dewi who became St. David, the Welsh patron saint.

While the civilizing influence of Christianity was making inroads, the country was far from settled. There were eighteen separate princedoms in this small area of 8,018 square miles (20,768 square kilometers). These princedoms, source of much warfare, also became the source of much Welsh pride and legend. These are the days that are celebrated by some as a golden age of heroic deeds, the age from which the bardic tradition springs.

Gradually, the numerous princedoms evolved—through treaties and intermarriage—into four kingdoms: Gwynedd in the north, Powys in the east, and Deheubarth and Morgannwg in the south.

The west and northwest coasts of Wales border on the Irish Sea.

A single language prevailed, a combination of Celtic and Latin; a single social system was based on kinship and the various rulers claimed a common ancestry.

Then came the threat from without. The Saxon "barbarians" who had overrun eastern Britain menaced the people of the west who began to call themselves *Cymry*, or compatriots. They, in turn, were called by the Saxons "wealas," meaning "foreigners." From this, obviously, came "Welsh" and "Wales." Some have linked these names to those given to other formerly Roman-dominated peoples: the Wallachians of Rumania, the Walachians of Greece, and the Walloons of Belgium.

During the time of Saxon menace, many left the Celtic western coast to go to Brittany, whence some of their ancestors had come. Throughout the sixth century many missionaries came to Wales from Brittany. This early interchange between the regions accounts for the fact that today Welsh people can go to Brittany and converse in, or at least understand, the Breton form of French.

Chapter 4

THE CENTURIES OF
CONQUEST

THE COMING OF THE NORMANS

By the middle of the ninth century, Wales was a distinct
country, effectively defined by Offa's Dyke, although politically it
still consisted of four kingdoms. There was a growing sense of
common culture and history. In the late eighth century, the
monks of St. David's monastery had started recording events—in
Latin. About 800, an obscure monk named Nennius, wrote, also in
Latin, his *History of the Britons*. Unfortunately for those who love
facts, this is a mix of wholly unreliable information reported from
Latin books and popular myth from oral sources.

In the next century there arose Hywel Dda who claimed to be
king of all Wales except the southeast. He seems to have been
accepted as such. It was he who issued the first Welsh coinage, in
his name. He is credited with codifying Welsh law, although none
of it was written down until the twelfth century. Welsh society at
this time was organized in pyramid form. At the top was the ruler
of a given territory, then various nobles, then freemen with rights
to grazing and arable land belonging to the group. Last came the
bondsmen who raised the crops, guarded the flocks, and generally

did all the dirty work. Most of them lived in hamlets huddled around the lord's household and some were so lowly in status that they could be sold along with the cattle they tended.

In the hundred twenty years after Hywel Dda's death in 850, there were thirty-five different Welsh rulers—all of whom died violently at the hands of Saxons, Danes, or their fellow Welsh. Thus, when the Normans arrived in Wales, the country was in no shape to withstand them. The Normans, who came from France, had, under their leader William the Conqueror, overpowered the Saxons in England in 1066. In five hundred years the Saxons had not been able to conquer the Welsh, but the Normans were a different breed. They quickly secured control of the main lines of entry into Wales, but the conquest was not complete until the fifteenth century.

The Normans were the greatest castle builders of all. They built twenty-five in Gwent alone and ringed the border with them. The castles were built to display Norman might and to intimidate the Welsh and many that stand today are still fearsome to behold. One of the most menacing is at Caerphilly in Glamorgan—a huge turreted edifice that is the second largest in all of Britain, second in size only to the royal family's Windsor Castle. It is one of the most powerful ever built in all of Europe.

The castle at Pembroke is considered by many to be the most impressive Norman castle of all. It has seven towers on its massive walls and an eighty-foot- (twenty-four-meter-) high keep built on the roof of an immense cavern called the Wogan. Here, in 1457, was born Henry Tudor who became Henry VII of England.

The Normans created earldoms to act as a buffer zone between the English and the more warlike Welsh. In particular, they established three great earldoms at Shrewsbury, Hereford, and

Two Norman castles, Pembroke (left) and Caerphilly (right)

Chester. These were not within Wales but on its borders and became known as the Marches. The kings of the four ancient kingdoms of Wales were all demoted to mere lords and had to be subservient to the Normans. Resistance to the overlords persisted but there was too much inner squabbling among the Welsh nobles for a successful general uprising. Slowly some of the "upper class" Welsh began to adapt to Norman ways. They began to build Norman-style castles for themselves. Also people began to benefit from the market towns created by the Normans. These brought an unprecedented bustle of trade that provided escape from agricultural drudgery to many formerly bound in servitude to landowners. These market towns usually clustered around a castle. You might enjoy reading about the construction of such a castle and about the activity that revolved around it in a wonderfully illustrated book by David Macauley. It is called *Castle* and a delightful TV program was made about it.

The Welsh who did not adjust to the Norman way of life were driven off to "Welshries" in the northern uplands, the craggy, harsh lands that the Normans did not want. There the Welsh preserved their traditional Celtic ways and lived by Welsh law. This region of Wales, Gwynedd, is still the staunchest enclave of Welsh nationalism.

Under the Normans, there was much resettlement of land and a consequent growth of the number of lawyers to cope with the complications of land rights. At this time the code of laws was written down for which Hywel Dda gets the credit. Not only laws were inscribed, but, for the first time, the epic poems, romances, and legendary tales that had been passed down by word of mouth. This flourishing of the written word was encouraged by the Cistercian monks who had followed the Normans from France. The oldest book in Welsh, *The Black Book of Carmarthen*, was produced in the late twelfth century at one of the Cistercian abbeys, Whitland in Carmarthenshire.

In 1136 there appeared *Historia Regum Brittaniae (History of the Kings of Britain)*, written in Latin by a cleric who had been born in Brittany but raised in Monmouth, and known as Geoffrey of Monmouth. His intent was to glorify the Welsh Celtic past. Unfortunately, he is no more reliable as a historian than was Nennius. As the modern Welsh historian A. H. Dodd writes in his *Short History of Wales*, Geoffrey's "main standby was his powerful imagination, whether exercised on mere embroidery or on sheer invention." However, as Professor Dodd says, Geoffrey's history became a best-seller. It was translated into Welsh and created a great deal of national pride. Even the Normans liked it, for it told of the legendary King Arthur and among the Normans there were many, like Geoffrey, from Brittany where Arthur was also a

Llywelyn the Great fought for independence, but was killed in 1282 (left). A monument (right) marks the spot in Powys.

popular legend. In Monmouth today you may be shown a certain window and be told that there Geoffrey sat to write his history. Many think this is as tall a tale as any Geoffrey ever told; but surely, he, of all people, would not object to a little truth-bending.

HOPES OF INDEPENDENCE

By the thirteenth century, the descendants of William the Conqueror had been succeeded on the throne of England by the Plantagenets who still spoke French, but were at home in England. It was in this century that the prospect of Welsh independence flourished and died and two great Welsh heroes arose.

The first of these was Llywelyn ab Iorwerth (known as Llywelyn the Great). He gained possession of the kingdom of Gwynedd and extended its limits over almost all of north Wales. He married the daughter of the English king John. This is the king whose barons in 1215 forced him to sign the Magna Carta, the most important document in English constitutional law. It set

41

limits to the king's power and was the foundation for the idea of due process of law. Llywelyn supported the barons against the king and it is said that the Magna Carta was actually drafted at Beaupre Castle in the Vale of Glamorgan. Three clauses in the charter were concerned with righting wrongs done to the Welsh. Llywelyn next presided over a council of Welsh princes and was acknowledged ruler of most of the country although pledging allegiance to the English king. He also strengthened his position by marrying his son and daughters into important Norman families.

The death of Llywelyn the Great, however, was followed by civil war and it was not until his grandson, Llywelyn ap Gruffydd (known as Llywelyn the Lost), took power that a measure of unity was restored. In 1267, the English king Henry III made a treaty declaring this Llywelyn to be Prince of Wales. Llywelyn soon rejected allegiance to the English king and, against express orders, built a castle and the beginnings of a town at Dolforwyn in Powys. This incurred the wrath of the English king Edward I who led two harsh invasions into Wales. Llywelyn did not have enough support in the country to withstand these onslaughts and when he was slain in 1282, the movement for independence collapsed.

THE DAYS OF ENGLISH OPPRESSION

Edward I's conquest of Wales brought about another round of castle building. The most formidable of these is Caernarfon Castle. Its massive 150-foot- (46-meter-) high turrets dominate the mouth of the river Seoint and look over to Anglesey. The site was carefully chosen, for it was here that the Welsh believed their

Left: Llywelyn's grave   Right: Caernarfon Castle, built by Edward I

Roman hero Macsen Wledig had planned a fortress and, indeed, had supposedly come home to die. By building a symbol of his own might on this revered site, Edward was visibly putting an end to Welsh dreams of glory.

At Caernarfon Castle, in 1301, Edward's first son was born and the custom began of designating the first son of the English monarch the Prince of Wales. It is said that Edward promised he would give the Welsh a new prince who did not speak English, implying he would speak Welsh. Instead they got a baby who could not speak at all.

For years after Edward's conquest of Wales, resistance to the English presence was mostly dormant. The country was administered at the top levels by the English but lesser posts could be held by Welsh. English common law gradually superseded the laws of Hywel Dda and the language of official business was either Latin or Norman French. While a Welsh "gentry" emerged and some sought their fortunes in London, resentment against the English smoldered, with occasional localized outbursts of revolt. The resentment still smolders. The Welsh and English still often do not trust one another. Although many English now live in

Wales, all year round or in weekend cottages, and although the Welsh have made their mark on English history—providing politicians and soldiers, not to mention the Tudor line of kings and queens—the nations have never been entirely comfortable with one another. Many of the castles that are so enchanting to tourists are, to the Welsh, constant reminders of English oppression.

Throughout the fourteenth century, Wales did not have a national identity. It had no central government but was ruled partly by the Prince of Wales, partly by various barons. It was an age of "castle government." Most castles were surrounded by boroughs where the Welsh were treated as second-class citizens and, for a long time, not allowed to acquire land or engage in trade.

The administration of the first Prince of Wales was not too harsh, and by the time he became Edward II he had a certain loyal following among the Welsh. For thirty-six years after he became king, there was no Prince of Wales. Edward III revived the title for his son, the Black Prince, who, when he set out to fight the French in 1346, took several thousand Welsh soldiers to fight with him. In the course of the next twenty-five years of war with the French, hundreds of thousands of Welsh joined the English army. This was a clever move on the part of the English to provide an outlet for Welsh warlike instincts and keep potential troublemakers well out of Wales.

Not only were men and taxes drained from Wales, but members of English noble households took over the highest positions in the Welsh church. Local discontent gradually swelled. It reached a climax when the English Parliament deposed Richard II, son of the Black Prince, who had a Welsh following.

Left: Edward I holds his son, Edward II, the first Prince of Wales Right: Owain Glyndwr

THE HEROIC OWAIN

At this time of widespread unrest the man who was to be the greatest Welsh hero entered the picture. This was Owain Glyndwr, a landowner in the Welsh Marches. Educated in England and having served in the English army, he was descended from princes of the old kingdoms of Powys and Deheubarth. A quarrel about land led him to attack his neighbor, the Lord of Ruthin, and this local incident developed into a national uprising.

Owain's feats of warfare became legendary. When his army defeated that of Henry IV as it advanced into Wales in 1402, tempestuous weather aided the Welsh, which was taken as a sign of Owain's supernatural power. (In Shakespeare's play *Henry IV, Part I*, Owain—here called Owen Glendower—says at one point; "I can call spirits from the vasty deep." To which his friend Hotspur replies: "Why, so can I, or so can any man;/ But will they come when you do call for them?")

Owain's forces twice failed in attacks on Caernarfon Castle but, after a long siege, did eventually capture another of Edward I's hated castles, the one at Harlech. Owain installed himself here with wife, family, and retainers and was acclaimed Prince of Wales. Here he held court. He summoned a parliament here and another in Machynlleth in north Powys. (On the supposed site of this parliament is now a museum of Welsh history with special attention to Owain's rebellion.) Owain made no small plans. He aimed to establish a Welsh archbishopric in the church and to found two universities. He captured Edmund Mortimer, an heir to the English throne, and married him to one of his daughters. He plotted to extend the frontier of Wales eastward into England. He brought high hope and a new national pride to Wales.

The strange fact is that this glorious hero did not go out in glory. His grand rebellion was not cruelly crushed, but simply dwindled away. The allies he thought he had in Scotland, Wales, and other parts of Europe did not really support him, his followers at home were lured away with promises of free pardon from the English king if they deserted Owain. This once victorious leader fought isolated guerrilla actions and then just gradually faded out. No one knows how or when he died. Thus he became more than a historical character. He became a myth, like Arthur, a king who would one day come again.

After the disappearance of Owain, the repressive hand of the English was visible everywhere in Wales. A few escaped it by joining the English king's army. Some won booty and knighthoods for their services and returned to set themselves up as important families. A few were able to infiltrate the boroughs and trades that had been up to that point exclusively occupied by the English.

Chapter 5

FROM THE TUDORS TO THE CIVIL WAR

THE HIGH HOPE OF THE TUDORS

In the fifteenth century, the Welsh were involved in the Wars of the Roses that raged in England between rival claimants to the throne from the noble houses of York and Lancaster. The House of York had supporters in the Marches and traced its claim through the Mortimers (remember Edmund Mortimer who married Owain's daughter?), while the Yorkish king Edward IV was a descendant of the daughter of Llywelyn the Great. The House of Lancaster was supported by the Welsh Tudor family. Edmund Tudor was married to the Lancastrian heiress and it was their son, Henry, who defeated Richard III at the Battle of Bosworth and who then became, in 1485, Henry VII—a Welsh-born, Welsh-speaking king of England! Not only that, but Owain had been related to the Tudors, which meant that the blood of the old hero flowed in Henry's veins! The Welsh were elated and saw visions of being at last in ascendancy over England, especially as the long period of political intrigue and warfare had weakened that country.

Left: Thomas Cromwell
Right: Henry VII

Henry did restore privileges that had been denied to the Welsh under the long English occupation. He appointed Welshmen to three important bishoprics in the church that formerly would have gone to Englishmen. He revived the title of Prince of Wales for his son whom he named Arthur, a gesture of symbolic importance because of the Welsh reverence for that name.

But Henry was really too busy establishing his right to the English throne to give much attention to Wales. Although many Welsh got appointments to the English court, they were by no means able to seize real power.

The famous Henry VIII, when Prince of Wales, never bothered to visit his principality. When he became king, feuding broke out between rival Welsh lords and between landowners and English bureaucrats. Henry was too entangled in his own quarrel with the pope over his divorce from his first wife to care about this. He did nothing except execute one of the warring lords, Rhys ap Gruffydd, who was popular enough to stir up a serious Welsh uprising if left alive. Thomas Cromwell, however, who became such a powerful and dreaded figure at Henry's court, decided to take Wales in hand. He clapped back many of the restrictions that Henry VII had removed and, through an intermediary, authorized thousands of executions in a few years.

THE PROSPECT OF UNITY

Then Cromwell changed his tactics. He was responsible for the Welsh Act of Union in 1536. This unified Wales politically, abolishing the Marches that had been the source of so much trouble. All Wales came under English common law and the Welsh were allowed to participate in their own government both locally and centrally. All this was not because Cromwell was suddenly smitten with kindheartedness, but because he did not want the Welsh to become so antagonistic that they might harbor foreigners bent on invading England to restore Papal authority which Henry had overthrown.

This was the age of the Reformation in Europe, begun in 1517 when Martin Luther first challenged the Catholic church. Henry had created the Anglican church and declared himself its head. Many of the Welsh had resented the greed of the clergy and so did not object to Henry's action. The Welsh gentry were not averse to snapping up the lands that were made available when Henry dissolved the monasteries. There is evidence from Welsh verse of this period that there was also much sorrow in the country at the desecration of so many churches.

During the short reign of Henry VIII's daughter Mary, Catholicism came back into favor but fell out of it again when Elizabeth I came to the throne in 1558. Wales was at the mercy of these changes in religion. To ensure that Protestantism would become firmly rooted in Wales, Elizabeth decreed that the Holy

During the reign of Queen Elizabeth I, the Bible was translated into Welsh. This ensured the continuance of the Welsh language.

Bible should be translated into Welsh. The New Testament appeared in 1567 and, in 1588, the translation was revised and the Old Testament added on by William Morgan, a farmer's son who became a bishop. This translation became a great cultural landmark. As the King James version of the Bible was to do later for the English language, William Morgan's Bible set the standard for the Welsh language and literature. It also ensured that the language would endure.

GLIMMERINGS OF PROSPERITY

By this time in the sixteenth century, life in Wales was considerably more peaceable than it had been. Prosperity became more popular than warfare and many Welsh, reconciled to the fact that they were not going to take over England, decided that they could at least make a decent living there so they went off for jobs in law, in public office, and in wealthy households. For those who stayed, sheep rearing was one very basic occupation and the raising of cattle increased. The Welsh drover, taking his herds to market in England, became a familiar figure. These men, who had

Sheep rearing has always been a basic occupation in Wales.

to be licensed to follow their trade, became important links with England and were often entrusted with carrying documents or money between the two countries. Some prospered and became bankers. The names of the banks they founded speak of the source of their owners' wealth. For instance, there was a Black Bullock Bank and a Black Sheep Bank. (Its one-pound note had a sheep engraved on it. The ten shilling note—a half pound—showed a lamb.) There are taverns called the Drovers Inn to be found all over Wales.

Because of all the sheep in Wales (there are still three times as many sheep as there are people), there was much spinning and weaving of their wool. At first this was done in farms and households, and later in mills, which by the nineteenth century were all over the place. In Elizabethan days, the wool was marketed across the border in the town of Shrewsbury and the middlemen were the ones who made most of the money. The

Livestock sales are still held in market towns founded by the Normans.

weavers did not get rich but at least they had a steady market and were able to supplement their meager farm incomes. The Welsh wool was coarse and thick and was sent abroad for such purposes as making red coats for the British army. It is said that the word "flannel" comes from the Welsh word for their wool: *gwlanen.*

The mining of lead, copper, gold, silver, coal, and slate was developed, mostly on local estates. Because roads were so bad at this time, coal and slate could not be easily transported inland so were used mainly for local needs. With increased industrial activity, however, Wales's seaports sprang into bustling life. Not only wool and metals, but grain and fish were exported to France and Ireland and even farther afield. At the same time, the old market towns founded by the Normans were coming back into their own. They are, to this day, the scene of livestock sales. But only 10 percent of the population (then not quite 300,000) lived in the ports and towns. The rest lived in the rural areas, as gentlemen with numerous retainers, as farmers of varying degrees of prosperity, and as poor farmworkers. It was a hard life for most.

Somehow, however, scholarship flourished. Dictionaries and grammars and treatises on the writing of poetry were produced, and at last a reliable history of Wales was published in 1584.

Oliver Cromwell (left), leader of the Roundheads, sent his men after King Charles I in Raglan Castle (right).

THE LAST INVASION

The mid-seventeenth century saw the last fighting on Welsh soil. In 1642 the Civil War broke out in England between the Royalists, or Cavaliers, who supported King Charles I, and the Parliamentarians— or Roundheads—who were led by Oliver Cromwell. At first, Wales was not involved beyond supporting the king with men and money and by having its cattle trade with London interrupted. Then, in 1644, a Roundhead force invaded Wales and established itself at Montgomery. The Welsh rallied to the Royalist side and rushed to fortify all those handy castles. Charles took refuge, for a time, in Raglan Castle in Gwent. Here he was pursued by Cromwell's men who inflicted severe damage on what had been the grandest castle in the area. A few castles, such as Caernarfon and Pembroke were strong enough to escape destruction although their defenders were forced to surrender; but many of the picturesque ruined castles in Wales today owe their sad state to the Civil War when they were, for the last time, scenes of bloody battles.

A Methodist church on the River Dee in Llangollen

Chapter 6
THE ROOTS OF
MODERN WALES

RELIGION

When the last cannon ceased fire in Wales, there were still non-military battles to be fought—for a decent living, for education, for preserving the language and the culture. The force that fired these struggles was religion.

The Welsh totally rejected the established Episcopalian church of England with its ceremonies, pomp, and bishops, and Wales became the great home of Nonconformism. Puritanism and Quakerism had both been welcomed there in the seventeenth century and the Methodist revival that swept parts of England in the eighteenth century took firm root in Wales. The Bible and the works of John Bunyan (who wrote *Pilgrim's Progress*) were the great educational factors. People wanted to learn to read so they could read these books.

Life revolved around the local chapel. These chapels, simple structures raised by the people, were the centers of learning, of social life, of the preservation of the language. They provided a feeling of solidarity that spilled over into politics. They were the source of the grand tradition of hymn singing.

One of two villages became particularly famous for their preachers. One of these, Daniel Rowlands (1713-1790) was a star attraction: people would walk or travel by boat from miles around to hear him preach at one of his revival meetings in the village of Langeitho in Cardiganshire. It is said that the famous composer Handel attended one of these meetings in 1739 and that the singing he heard there of a certain hymn inspired him to write the Hallelujah Chorus in his great work *The Messiah.*

Today, the heyday of the chapel is long past. Religion is no longer the guiding force it once was. The battle for education is long over, and all kinds of modern distractions are available to provide social life. The movement of people away from little settlements to larger towns has also shifted the center of their interests to the larger community. The chapel, too, was in many ways a repressive influence, frowning on those who did not behave in a completely respectable manner. As the Welsh have always had a strain of high-spiritedness in their nature, with a love of drinking, sport, and merrymaking, there were always those who found the demands of the chapel too strict.

Although the Welsh have been so strongly Nonconformist, they have never persecuted those of other beliefs. There are a few members of the Church of England. There are Catholics, particularly among the many who have emigrated from Ireland in search of work. There have been Jewish people in Wales since Roman times. There was a Jewish mayor in Swansea as early as 1840 and, in 1910—when there was much anti-Semitic feeling in the English Parliament—Swansea elected a Jewish Liberal member of Parliament (or M.P.). Jews have fitted easily into Welsh life. At one time, there were those of the Welsh who considered themselves to be the Lost Tribe of Israel.

EDUCATION

Education is greatly prized in Wales. In the past it was often very hard to come by, and had, to a good extent, to be self-education. There are many instances of working people—colliers, quarrymen, and farmers—who, with little formal schooling, read voraciously and even acquired libraries of their own.

The great educational influence in Wales in the eighteenth and nineteenth centuries was the Sunday schools. (Their forerunners were the Circulating Schools founded by Griffith Jones of Llanddower [1683-1761]. Through his efforts, more than 150,000 people from age six to seventy were taught to read the Bible in Welsh.) The Sunday schools were founded by Thomas Charles of Bala (1755-1814). They taught children to read and write and adults to study and discuss serious theological and philosophical subjects. They reached their peak in the nineteenth century and in some parts of Wales were the only schools available. In certain areas, education was provided by the British and Foreign Schools Society, founded in 1808, and the National Schools Society, founded in 1811. The latter was under the control of the clergy and attendance at church on Sunday was part of the curriculum.

In 1847, a commission to investigate the state of schools in Wales was set up. It came up with a 1,183-page report (as commissions are apt to do) and it strongly condemned the use of the Welsh language in schools and the influence of the Nonconformist chapel. As is usual with such reports, it made a lot of people angry, but it did expose many school defects such as unsatisfactory buildings and sanitation and poorly trained teachers.

Even before this report, there had been prejudice against

University College, founded at Aberystwyth in 1872, is on Cardigan Bay.

speaking Welsh in schools and there existed an infamous implement called the Welsh Not. This was a four-inch (ten-centimeter) slab of wood with the words "Welsh Not" carved on it. This was handed to the first pupil caught speaking Welsh on any day and that pupil then had to inform on any other offenders. They were all lined up at the end of the day and beaten with a cane.

In 1870 a new Education Act, passed in England, brought better schools to Wales. Many fine primary schools were established then that still exist today. Compulsory school attendance was introduced in 1880. Today Welsh schools are under local control where attendance is required through age sixteen, although many students go on to higher education. Comprehensive schools, teaching both academic and vocational subjects, are common now. The one established on the island of Anglesey in 1952 was the first of this kind in all of Great Britain. Far from being banned, the Welsh language is widely taught, even to children whose parents do not speak it at home.

The University of Wales at Cardiff

Wales was long deprived of higher education, too. It was not until 1872 that a University College was founded at Aberystwyth. The money to start it was raised from Welsh people at home and abroad and from other sympathizers. In 1893, it became the University of Wales, with power to grant its own degrees. It now has branches in Bangor, Cardiff, Swansea, and Lampeter. There are also several theological colleges, technical colleges, colleges of art, agriculture, drama, and music, and a Welsh National College of Medicine. In a beautiful medieval castle at St. Donat's in the Vale of Glamorgan is the United World College (established in 1962 as Atlantic College). Here more than three hundred students gather from all over the world.

Ever since the old days of the Sunday Schools, the adult education movement in Wales has grown steadily. In 1929, Harlech College became the first residential college for adults, providing a liberal arts education that enabled many of the students to graduate to further university training. The Open

University, which provides courses for adults all over Britain, is very popular in Wales. The Workers' Educational Association, founded in 1903, has played a very important part in many Welsh lives as have the extramural departments at the university colleges. It is claimed that, by 1955, these departments were offering adult education to a larger proportion of people than were any other such systems in Great Britain. In the 1920s there was also a thriving National Council of Labour Colleges founded to serve the needs of workers in South Wales. It provided some excellent classes, but its volunteer teachers had a decidedly Marxist bias.

POLITICS

Wales is technically a principality, with a Prince of Wales. Although the present prince is the only one who has ever taken the trouble to learn some Welsh and although he and his wife make state visits there, he does not govern Wales. Wales is governed by the British Parliament and there is a Secretary of State for Wales in London and a Welsh office for official business in Cardiff. Wales elects members to the Parliament in London. In fact, it does so with enthusiasm, having the highest turnout in elections of any place in Britain.

Because of conditions during the Industrial Revolution and the prolonged exploitation of the workers in various heavy industries, Wales developed a strong working-class consciousness, first with radical liberal sympathies and then socialist ones. In 1900, Keir Hardie (who happened to be a Scot) was elected to Parliament as the first Labour M.P. by a Welsh coal-mining constituency.

Many Welsh have made their mark in Parliament, but the most

Keir Hardie was elected to Parliament as the first Labour M.P.

famous by far is David Lloyd George (1863-1945). He was a Liberal M.P. from 1890-1945, Chancellor of the Exchequer from 1908-1915, and Prime Minister from 1916-1922. For the first two years of this period, World War I was still raging and Lloyd George is credited with the reorganization of the munitions industry that was essential to the Allies to win the war. In his long career he achieved much. In 1909, as Chancellor of the Exchequer, he produced the People's Budget, which raised taxes from the rich and laid the foundation for the future welfare state. In 1911, he designed the first comprehensive health and unemployment insurance plan. Naturally, this made him enemies as well as friends.

A charming man, with the Welsh gift for oratory, he was small of stature but had a flamboyant appearance. He delighted

A photograph of David Lloyd George (left) and a cartoon (right) depicting him as the Welsh Wizard

cartoonists especially, with his flowing hair and mustache and twinkling eyes. He usually wore a cloak and wide-brimmed hat and was known—sometimes affectionately, sometimes not—as the Welsh Wizard. In the little village of Llanystumdwy in north Wales you can see the cottage where he was raised and, nearby, the estate—now a museum—that he bought in later life. His daughter Megan followed his footsteps into politics, becoming one of the first women to be elected to Parliament.

Next to Lloyd George, the most colorful Welsh politician has been Aneurin Bevan, born in 1890 and a Labour M.P. from 1929 until his death in 1960. When the Labour party came into power in 1945, he became Minister of Health, a position he held until 1951. Bevan grew up in a mining community (he worked down the pit at age thirteen) and had been well aware of the silicosis, tuberculosis, and other diseases that afflicted miners. His village of Tredegar had been the first, in the 1890s, to establish a Workers Medical Aid Society. (A.J. Cronin, who became a novelist, was one of the doctors who worked for this society in the 1920s and he

Aneurin Bevan served for thirty-one years as a member of Parliament. As Minister of Health he succeeded in providing good medical care for all citizens.

wrote about the battle to defeat silicosis in his novel *The Citadel*, which was dramatized on TV's Masterpiece Theater.)

In 1923, Bevan was elected to the Hospital Committee that worked with the Society; so, thirty-two years later, in 1955, when he was able as Minister of Health to launch the British National Health Service, he was fulfilling a lifelong ambition to make good medical attention available to all.

The tide of Welsh Nationalism has been rising in recent years. The nationalist movement *Plaid Cymru* was established in 1925 and sent its first M.P. to London in 1966. Many extremists are to be found in the Welsh Language Society and they foment such very real grievances as the facts that half the water produced in the Welsh hydroelectric system goes to England and that production in Wales has exceeded that in the rest of Britain while personal income has been lower and unemployment higher.

The anti-nuclear movement is strong in Wales. The celebrated sit-in (which has been going on for years) protesting the presence of the United States missile base at Greenham Common in England was first started by a group of women from Wales.

*A farmhouse (above) near Cader Idris and
the Iron Works Museum (below) at Blaenavon*

Chapter 7

THE WELSH AT WORK

INDUSTRY IN THE PAST

The story of Welsh industry is all too largely "once upon a time." Seventy-three percent of Welsh land is used for agriculture now, and 11 percent of the remainder is woodland or forest. Tourism is a thriving business because of the beauty of the country and the fascination of all those castles and legends. The remains of many industries have been turned into tourist attractions; museums now mark the spots where thousands once worked. These were not the "good old days," however, as the working conditions were often harsh or horrendous and, when the industries were at their peaks, it was not the Welsh worker who got rich but the owners who often were not Welsh.

The woolen trade was one of the busiest. The tradition of weaving and spinning goes back to the middle ages and, in Elizabethan days, both men and women knitted woolen stockings constantly—they even knitted while walking around. Elizabeth I, indeed, did much for the trade by making the wearing of the "Monmouth cap" compulsory on Sundays and holy days. In the nineteenth century, factories replaced home looms and trade was brisk. Now only a few mills still operate and produce mainly for tourists. Welsh tweed is heavy and thick and has not caught the world's fancy in the way Scottish tweed has.

Gold and silver have been mined in Wales since Roman days as have lead and copper. The Parys Mountain copper mine in Anglesey was the most productive in all the world in the eighteenth century. Ships from the British, French, Dutch, and Spanish fleets were copper bottomed, clad with copper from the Parys mine. Parys became both a boom town and an industrial horror story as its air became more and more polluted.

In the nineteenth century, slate quarrying was a healthy industry. Houses all over the British empire, America, and Europe were roofed with Welsh slate. The quarrymen were a special breed; not only were they skilled workers but avid readers, lovers of intellectual discussion, and even poets. They were a clannish lot, with whole families of men working together and a strong bond of brotherhood between the families. There is still a little slate quarrying in Gwynedd and in gift stores all over Wales are charming examples of slate crafts—boxes, ashtrays, and pins, etc., with delicate carving on the slate. Several disused quarries are open to view. One of the largest, Dinworic Quarry, once employed three thousand people in the early 1900s. It closed completely in 1969 after a long period of dwindling business and is now the Welsh Slate Museum where much of the original machinery is on display.

While there had been a few small ironworks in south Wales as early as the sixteenth century, the great ironworks that scarred the beautiful valleys of Glamorgan and Gwent were developed in the late eighteenth century. By the early nineteenth century, the town of Merthyr Tydfil in Gwent was the largest iron producer in the

The roofs of the houses in Conwy (left) may have come from the slate quarry (right) in Llanberis.

world. Near there, at a town called Blaenavon, you can still see one of the huge ironworks, now a museum. There are the old furnaces, the workers' cottages, and the Big Pit, one of the oldest mines in Wales. You can descend 300 feet (91 meters) in a cage and see where so many thousands toiled under dreadful conditions. You can offer thanks that you are seeing this just as a tourist, for chances are you would have been working down there had you lived hereabouts a hundred years or so ago. The mine was an equal opportunity employer of men, women, and children.

Coal was the other major industry in Wales. At the end of the nineteenth century, the formerly quiet and pastoral Rhondda Valley had a population of 115,000; 40,000 miners worked in the pits. For two hundred years, life in rural Wales had been very grim, with crop failures and people driven off the land when landlords enclosed for their own use what had been considered common land. So the new industries looked tempting and the wages seemed high to those who had been starving.

Welsh coal miners, like slate quarrymen, were a close-knit group. Those who worked together also went to the same chapel

A town in the old coal mining area of South Wales

and had the same desire for education. Their community of
interest and the shared danger of their work made them comrades
and the South Wales Miners Federation, formed after a bitter
strike in 1898, was one of the great movements for working class
solidarity.

The heavy industries in Wales flourished during the World
War I years (1914-1918), except for the slate industry that
slumped with the decline in house building. The prosperity did
not last, however, and the Great Depression devastated Wales.
One-fifth of the population was unemployed by 1932. Many left
to try to find work in England. After a temporary lift during
World War II, Welsh industry in general has slowed so that there
is again widespread unemployment. The last pit in the once-
booming Rhondda Valley closed in July 1986.

So what do the Welsh do now for a living?

INDUSTRY TODAY

Farming still endures. Cattle rearing is thriving and the milk
business is well-organized and efficient. Millions of gallons of

A modern nuclear power plant (left) contrasts with fishermen (right) using their traditional coracles.

milk are collected from countless little farms and shipped off to markets as far away as London. Sheep rearing prospers. The ancient trade of fishing is still followed and, in a few rivers, is done from age-old little boats called coracles, which look like a half a walnut shell constructed of willow and hazel boughs covered with hide.

There are many service industries such as construction and gas and electricity production. The southwest ports that used to export so much mineral wealth now import iron ore, general cargo, and oil. Milford Haven in Dyfed has become a major port for supertankers and there are oil refineries nearby. Much of the oil for these refineries comes by pipeline from the North Sea. The British Royal Mint is at Llantrisant in Glamorgan and all documents concerning automobiles are processed in Swansea.

Many who live in the pleasant little towns and villages throughout the country depend for a considerable part of their livelihood on tourism, which is in some places resented as much as it is welcomed. A proud nation does not like to think that it is just some quaint showplace.

EMIGRATION OF WELSH

In their long history of struggle to make a living, many Welsh have had to go abroad. (Remember, that to the Welsh, England is abroad.) Apart from those who for centuries went to war, there were those who followed the Tudors over the border. Many in the seventeenth century sought religious freedom in America, and Pennsylvania, in particular, drew Welsh immigrants. At the end of the eighteenth century, an attempt was made to found a Welsh utopia in western Pennsylvania and although this was not realized, the legacy is to be found in names like Bryn Mawr. This settlement was to be called Cambria, an ancient name for Wales, derived from the Cambrian Mountains. Others went to Oneida in New York state where many Welsh chapels were founded and where people of Welsh descent still meet. There was another unsuccessful attempt to establish a settlement in Tennessee.

The greatest influx of Welsh to North America was in the nineteenth century when coal miners and steel workers came to seek their fortunes in Pennsylvania. Before the century ended there were five thousand native Welsh people in Scranton, two thousand in Wilkes Barre, and three thousand in Pittsburgh. The tinplate industry was peopled largely by Welsh. Among the mining families that came to Pennsylvania were the parents of John L. (Llewellyn) Lewis. He became the famous leader of the miners in America and was president of the United Mine Workers from 1920-1960.

A COLONY OF THEIR OWN

The Welsh who first went to North America dreamed of founding a Welsh-speaking, chapel-going community, but those

John L. Lewis, the son of Welsh immigrants, was a famous American labor leader in the mining industry.

who came later were quickly assimilated. The dream was finally realized in South America in an unlikely region of Argentina, in the mostly desert area of Patagonia. Among the first settlers who arrived there in 1865 were only two farmers (and three ministers), but gradually the land was irrigated and made into productive farmland. Despite all kinds of setbacks and troubles (including a murderous visit from Butch Cassidy and the Sundance Kid), *Y Wladfa*—the Colony—took hold. As more settlers arrived from Wales, another community was established deep in the Andes mountains where sheep were successfully raised. This was known as *Cym Hyfryd*, the Lovely Valley.

For years these settlers followed strict Welsh traditions, speaking nothing but Welsh. Both men and women had equal political rights and the economy was run on a cooperative basis. To this day, although more Spanish than Welsh is spoken, more than five thousand people are bilingual in Spanish and Welsh and there are thirteen all-Welsh churches. The English novelist Bruce Chatwin wrote a delightful travel book, *In Patagonia*, showing how the Welshness of the region is still there.

There are Welsh people in many different parts of the world including Australia, where many were transported years ago for such sins as stirring up protests about living conditions and unjust taxes. One state in Australia is called New South Wales.

Scenes of Cardiff, clockwise from above, are: Cardiff Castle, fountains near the law courts, the Welsh Folk Museum, and public transportation passing Cardiff Castle in the center of town.

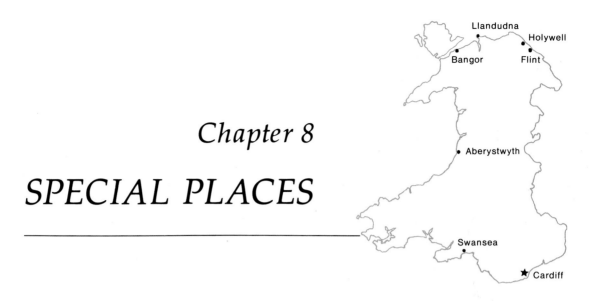

Chapter 8

SPECIAL PLACES

CARDIFF, THE CAPITAL

The capital of Wales is Cardiff (in Welsh, *Caerdydd*), with a population of about 300,000. Very few people speak Welsh although a Celtic film festival is held there. But then Cardiff is full of contrasts. A centuries-old castle stands right in the middle of town on a busy street corner with buses whizzing by. Although Wales is administered from London, its City Center, set on a sixty-acre (twenty-four hectare) site near the castle, would not be out of place in a major capital city. In the City Hall is the magnificent Marble Hall containing statues of Wales's great heroes. Here, too, is the splendid National Museum of Wales with its collection of fine Welsh paintings and exhibits of Welsh crafts, history, and ways of life throughout the centuries.

Cardiff stands on the river Taff. (The name Taffy is sometimes used in England to refer to a Welsh person, but this is not looked on kindly in Wales.) At the height of the Industrial Revolution, Cardiff was a major port, sending iron ore, steel, and coal around the world. The city still seems bustling and prosperous today,

City Hall (left) and Civic Center (right) in Cardiff

complete with a modern shopping center. But Cardiff makes its living now mainly in service trades. The once vital dockyard areas no longer are the hub of commerce; the Museum of Maritime Affairs stands on what was once a teeming center of activity.

In Cardiff is a branch of the University of Wales and the Welsh College of Music and Drama. Its New Theater and St. David's Hall hold performances by leading dance and drama groups, symphony orchestras and, of course, the Welsh National Opera.

Large areas of Cardiff are parkland and in one of these is the National Sports Center. The Glamorgan Cricket Ground is there; the Cardiff Rugby Club and the National Rugby Stadium are nearby. There is a Cardiff City Football (soccer) Club, and Cardiff also is one of the few places in the United Kingdom where baseball is played regularly.

Cardiff Castle is an amazing place. There it sits in the middle of a modern town containing evidence of several centuries of history. There are traces of a Roman fort built more than 1,900 years ago. There is an eleventh-century Norman keep, an old fortress that is the nucleus of the whole structure. As the castle

A panoramic view of Cardiff showing the National Rugby Stadium

passed from family to family through hundreds of years of often bloodstained history, the owners ventured out of the old uncomfortable keep and built additions on the outer walls of the compound. More comfortable living quarters were constructed as were towers and halls to display the power and wealth of the owners. In the eighteenth century the castle came into the possession of a Scottish family, the Butes. The heir to the then Marquess of Bute was created Baron Cardiff in 1776.

The Bute family grew enormously rich during the Industrial Revolution. They owned not only coal mines but the shipping lines that transported the coal. One whole section of Cardiff was known as Butetown. The Butes made various embellishments to the castle and it was the third Marquess of Bute, in the nineteenth century, who raised it to its present splendor. He commissioned the most famous architect/designer of the day, William Burges, to decorate the living quarters of the castle. And decorate it he did.

A ceiling in Cardiff Castle (left) and the annual Searchlight Tattoo (right)

The result is a breathtaking display of what is known as high Victorian art at its very highest. There are rooms full of intricate carving, ceilings inlaid with gold, ornate furniture set with ivory and jewels, marvelously tiled floors and walls, an enchanting roof garden, and elaborate murals depicting historical events. Perhaps feeling that all this was too much of a good thing, the Bute family gave the castle and its grounds to the city of Cardiff in 1947. The elegant banquet hall may now be rented for important dinners or lavish wedding receptions.

Thousands of tourists flock through this castle staring, in varying degrees of awe, shock, or disapproval, at all the extravagance of decoration. Sometimes the tour guide's commentary is drowned out by the shrieks of peacocks who strut around the gardens outside clamoring to be fed by the tourists who are basking in the castle gardens.

There is an annual Searchlight Tattoo (floodlit military exercise) held on the grounds of the castle and the castle and keep are a magical sight. It is doubtful if the peacocks approve, however.

The center of Swansea

SWANSEA

Swansea, not far west of Cardiff on the Bristol Channel, is the only other large town in Wales. Its population is over 170,000 and it was officially promoted from "town" to "city" by Prince Charles when he became Prince of Wales in 1969. Like all seafaring towns, it has always had a cosmopolitan air and has absorbed many foreigners.

It is the place in which poet Dylan Thomas was born; he described it as an "ugly lovely town." Much of the center of the town that Dylan knew was destroyed by World War II bombs, but the long and splendidly-curving shore still offers a marvelous prospect to the pleasant Edwardian terraced houses that overlook it. Swansea Bay was once judged by the Victorian writer Walter Savage Landor to be more beautiful than the Bay of Naples, the supreme compliment he could pay it. (A century before in the mid-1800s, he could not have made this statement; for Swansea was the center of the world's copper industry and the pollution in

The Industrial and Maritime Museum

the area was so horrendous that all plant life died and no birds flew near the place.)

The center of town was rebuilt after World War II and has a fine modern shopping center. There are not many impressive buildings, except for the Guildhall, which is distinguished by a spectacular display of murals by Welsh artist Frank Brangwyn. The Industrial and Maritime Museum is well worth a visit. It includes a fully working woolen mill.

Swansea is an enjoyable town to live in, with plenty of park space and entertainment of all kinds including, of course, musical events. Its industry is all situated east of the town, so it seems much like a seaside resort and many people come there on vacation. At one end of Swansea Bay stands a magnificent headland known as the Mumbles where the oyster trade flourishes. Oyster beds have been cultivated in this area since Roman times. In 1807, a railway line—with horse-drawn carriages!—was established between Swansea and the Mumbles.

Hotels line the seafront in Aberystwyth.

This is said to have been the first-ever public passenger line in Britain. The horses were replaced by steam engines in 1877 and the railway, alas, no longer exists.

ABERYSTWYTH

Aberystwyth is an important town in Wales, although not a big one. It is the site of the main branch of the University of Wales and, when the students are gone, its population is only about ten thousand. It lies almost exactly in the center of the west coast of Wales, on beautiful Cardigan Bay surrounded by beautiful countryside. When the students depart for their summer vacation, in come flocks of tourists to occupy the charming hotels lining the seafront. At one end of the town is a headland called Constitution Hill, which has a quaint little funicular railway. At the other end of the town, on another headland, can be seen one of the largest Iron Age forts in all of Wales and, nearby, the ruins of one of Edward I's castles, now surrounded by a lovely formal garden.

The National Library of Wales

Aberystwyth houses the national Library of Wales. This is a copyright library like the Library of Congress in Washington, D.C., and the British Museum in London, which means copies of each book published in the country must be sent there. It has many priceless books and manuscripts, including *The Black Book of Carmarthen*, the oldest book written in Welsh, and an original copy of the *Mabinogion*, the collection of Welsh legends.

Close by Aberystwyth is the lovely Rheidol Valley. Its chief attraction for tourists is the Devil's Bridge, which spans a series of waterfalls in a deep, mysterious, wooded ravine where the river Rheidol joins the river Mynach. The swirling waters under the bridge are called the Devil's Punchbowl.

There is, of course, a legend about this bridge. They say that a poor old woman, whose cow was stranded on the wrong side of the flooded river Mynach, was regarding it in despair when a voice behind her said, "Can I help?" She turned to see a monk standing there. He offered to build her a bridge if she would give him the first living thing that crossed it. She agreed but, waiting in

St. Deiniol Cathedral in Bangor

her cottage, she grew suspicious. When the monk announced very soon that the bridge was ready, she brought out a crust of bread and her little black dog. She threw the crust across the bridge, the dog trotted after it and the "monk" who had been expecting the cow, vanished in a rage and a cloud of smoke. The devil, obviously.

OTHER PLACES

Bangor, in the northwest is another university town. It is also a good starting-off place for tourists, being only 2.5 miles (4 kilometers) from the Menai Straits Bridges leading to Anglesey. It has a tiny cathedral, St. Deiniol, and a most interesting Bible Garden. This contains every tree, plant, and flower mentioned in the Bible—every one, that is, that can survive the local climate.

Near Bangor is Penrhyn Castle, constructed like a Norman castle with turrets, battlements, a portcullis, etc., but actually built in 1827-1840 by a rich industrialist who owned slate quarries in

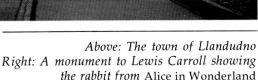

Above: The town of Llandudno
Right: A monument to Lewis Carroll showing
the rabbit from Alice in Wonderland

Gwynedd. Its main bedroom contains a monstrous four-poster bed made of slate that was built for Queen Victoria's use during a visit. (She took one look at it and decided—no thanks.) There is also a museum in this castle that houses (besides the famous railway sign) locomotives, stuffed birds and animals, and more than one thousand dolls from all over the world.

Not too far east of Bangor is Llandudno, which has been a popular resort since the mid-1800s. In 1862, Charles Dodgson went there to spend a vacation with the Liddell family. It was for young Alice Liddell that Dodgson—whom you know as Lewis Carroll—wrote *Alice in Wonderland* and there is a memorial to him in the town. The beauty of Llandudno is set off between two impressive headlands known as Great Ormes Head and Little Ormes Head.

Also in north Wales, in the east near the town of Flint, is Holywell, a small industrial town where the woolen trade is still carried on. Its chief fame, however, comes from the spot from which it takes its name—a holy well believed to have healing

waters. Legend has it that a lovely young girl, Winifred, rejected
the advances of a brutal prince who flew into a rage and cut off
her head. Her uncle then restored her head to her body and, in the
place where she had been beheaded, a spring of water
miraculously burst forth. In the fifteenth century, a well was built
over the spring, now known as the shrine of St. Winifred. It has
been called "the Lourdes of Wales" and pilgrims have flocked
there for more than a thousand years.

THE GREAT LITTLE TRAINS

The Welsh have always loved trains since they first appeared on
the scene. Trains not only were quickly adopted by travelers,
while in other parts of Britain people were afraid of the puffing
monsters, but they became a valuable part of the economy making
it possible to transport coal, slate, and other materials not so easily
moved before. The great railroad age has passed here, as
elsewhere, but the Welsh have not parted willingly with their

Above: The Brecon Mountain Railway
Below: The Snowdon Mountain Railway at the mountain summit

trains and many have been resurrected as a grand tourist attraction. These are the "Great Little Trains of Wales." There are thirteen of them, running on narrow-gauge lines and mostly powered by steam or a mixture of steam and diesel oil. They chug through some of the most scenic parts of Wales and are all great fun to ride.

In the Snowdonia area are the Snowdon Mountain Railway, which goes to the mountain summit; the Ffestinog Railway; the Llanberis Railway; and the Welsh Highland Railway, which is operated entirely by volunteers (think of all the people who always wanted to be engine drivers!). Another volunteer-operated line is the Talyllyn Railway, which goes from the town of Tywyn on the coast of Merioneth to a charming little lake at the foot of Cader Idris.

The Welshpool and Llanfair Railway, passing through lovely woodland scenery on the borders of Powys, uses steam engines from Austria, Africa, and the West Indies. In Powys is the Bala Lake Railway that goes along the shore of the largest natural lake in Wales. The Vale of Rheidol Railway is the last wholly steam operated railway belonging to the national company, British Railways. It goes from Aberystwyth to Devil's Bridge. Fairbourne Railway is the littlest of the little, running for only two miles along a stretch of Cardigan Bay. The Brecon Mountain Railway goes through the spectacular scenery of the Brecon Beacons.

Rounding out the set are: the Great Orme Tramway from Llandudno, a cable car; the Aberystwyth Cliff Railway, a funicular cable car; and the Llechwedd Slate Caverns Tramway, an electric train that runs underground into an old slate mine where visitors can see how slate miners worked by candlelight in Victorian days.

Part of the national anthem of Wales reads: "The land of my Fathers
so dear to my soul,/The land which the poet and mistrel extol."

Chapter 9

THE SOUL OF WALES

POETRY AND POETS

To the Welsh, poetry has always been a part of life. From earliest times, poets known as *bards* chronicled the events of the day. When princes held court throughout the land, each had his resident bard, and some of the princes were themselves poets. These bards were the poets laureate of the courts, celebrating feats of battle, the power of the princes, and important happenings of court life. They were, in a way, propagandists for the princes. They were also very professional, studying the composition of poetry as a craft with special skills and regulations. They were honored figures both in the courts and the surrounding communities.

Although the nature of poetry has changed and developed in Wales throughout the centuries, the poet has remained a respected figure. It is centuries, however, since poets have been a social elite. They have come from all walks of life: they have been miners, farmers, preachers, teachers, or doctors. They have continued to comment on events around them and have never hesitated to be political, writing poems about such topics as the evils of industry,

Welsh poets have written about the evils of industry.

the Great Depression, and the condition of the miners. One of the most ardent Welsh nationalists today is poet Saunders Lewis.

Unfortunately for the rest of the world some of the greatest Welsh poets have written only in Welsh; even when translations have been made, much of the original grandeur has been lost. There have been many, however, who have written in English.

The earliest widely known Welsh poets writing in English lived in the seventeenth century and belonged to the group known as metaphysical poets, who wrote mostly about spiritual matters. They were George Herbert (1593-1633), Thomas Vaughan (1621-1666), and Henry Vaughan (1621-1695).

W. H. Davies (1871-1940) was a fine lyric poet who spent a great deal of his life in America, including a spell of gold prospecting in the Klondike. His best-known work is not, however, a poem but his *Autobiography of a Super-Tramp*, a splendid adventure story.

World War I aroused the passions of many poets, among them the Welshman Wilfred Owen. He was born in 1895 and killed in battle just one week before the Armistice on November 11, 1918. He left behind many beautiful but bitter poems about the futility of war. These poems were set to music by the famous British composer Benjamin Britten in "War Requiem," written for the dedication in 1962 of the new Coventry Cathedral, which replaced the old one bombed by the Germans in World War II.

Alun Lewis was the Welsh poet of World War II. Born into a mining family in 1915, he trained as a teacher but had to go into the army and was killed in Burma in 1944. His most famous poem, "All Day It Has Rained," is one that strikes a chord in anyone who has ever been cold and wet and miserable in an army camp.

The most famous Welsh poet is, of course, Dylan Thomas (1914-1953). He was born in Swansea, the seaport town that he wrote about in many poems and stories. His father was a schoolteacher who read Shakespeare to Dylan from an early age, and named him Dylan from a character in the collection of Welsh legends, the *Mabinogion.*

Dylan Thomas spoke no Welsh—something for which many of his countrymen did not forgive him. His poetry is much admired for the imagery of such lines as: "Of the star-gestured children in the park." This is from a poem written about Cwmdonkin Park in Swansea where he used to play as a boy. There is a monument to him there now around which, appropriately, children play. His most famous lines are those he wrote when his father was dying: "Do not go gentle into that good night/ Rage, rage against the dying of the light."

Dylan worked first in Swansea as a journalist and went to London at the age of twenty. He immediately plunged into the literary life. He had early success with his poems and later became a popular broadcaster on the British Broadcasting Corporation's radio programs. He was enormously popular, too, as a drinking companion and a great conversationalist. He followed a pattern of wild spending, however, and was forever borrowing money from

Left: Dylan Thomas directing a performance of "Under Milk Wood"
Right: From the portrait of Dylan Thomas by Augustus John

his friends. His wife Caitlin and his children suffered much from his spendthrift habits and were happy only when he retreated to Wales, as he did from time to time, to write poetry.

Although Dylan often railed against the narrowness of Welsh life, he always loved the land and, after his death on a last disastrous trip to America—where he was adored on college campuses—he was brought home to be buried at Laugharne.

Among his most enduring writings are the delightful "A Child's Christmas in Wales," which is read every Christmastime on British radio; and *Under Milk Wood*, a much performed radio play, which was also made into a film for television starring Richard Burton and Elizabeth Taylor.

Much less widely known than Dylan Thomas is Vernon Watkins who was his longtime friend, supporting him with both encouragement and cash. Watkins, too, grew up in Swansea where he worked most of his life in a bank. The two did not meet until after the publication of Dylan's first collection of poems when he was twenty-one and Watkins twenty-nine. Watkins

The Welsh enjoy music.

published several volumes of poems much admired by fellow poets and, in later years taught in America at the University of Washington in Seattle.

MUSIC AND MUSICIANS

Music is dear to the hearts of the Welsh—particularly singing. Not only are there many famous singers, from opera stars such as Margaret Price, Gareth Evans, and Geraint Evans to pop singers such as Tom Jones and Shirley Bassey, but ordinary folk burst into song at any good excuse. Rugby matches, for instance, are great occasions for loud, emotional mass singing of the best-known Welsh hymns *"Cym Rhondda"* and "Land of Our Fathers."

The passion for hymn singing springs from the tradition of Methodist chapel going which, for so long, was often the only break in the monotony of a grindingly hardworking life. Nowadays, when TV and movies and other modern pleasures are readily available in Wales, the love of hymn singing endures.

Where other nations have merry drinking songs, the Welsh, when they congregate in taverns, sing hymns.

Welsh choirs—particularly huge male voice choirs—are celebrated and many have traveled abroad to the United States and elsewhere. Some of the best of these choirs were groups of coal miners. During the Great Depression when unemployment in the Welsh mines was especially bad, many miners went to London and sang in the streets to bring their plight to the attention of the public and the government. It was an early form of "Live Aid" that, unfortunately, did not raise much money but may have stirred a few consciences.

From the mines, too, came many of the brass bands, which are so beloved of the Welsh and which are a cheerful feature of any good *eisteddfod* (poetry, dance, music competition). The Welsh National Opera Company was founded by Idloes Owen who, before he became a professional musician, was a miner.

The great musical instrument of Wales is the harp. It has been part of the culture for as long as recorded history. It was played in the castles of the nobility and among ordinary people. It is a strange fact that many of the most celebrated harpists, down the centuries, have been blind. The best-known modern male harpist is Osian Ellis. There have also been many acclaimed women harpists such as today's Eleanor Bennett Owen, Mair Jones, and Ann Griffith.

Many Welsh composers, unfortunately, have been unknown beyond Wales. Most of them were not able to support themselves without also working in quarries or mines and there was no formal musical education available. Now, with better economic and educational circumstances, with opportunities on radio and television, and with the founding in 1954 of the Guild for the

Wales's greatest musical instrument is the harp (center) and some of her well-known musicians are Ivor Novello (left), who composed and starred in operettas, and Sir Geraint Evans (right), an international opera star.

Promotion of Welsh Music, such composers as Grace Williams, Alun Hoddinett, and William Mathias are able to gain the attention of a wider public.

The composer best known to the outside world in the early twentieth century was one who did not meet with approval from those interested in the higher forms of music. This was Ivor Novello, a classically handsome man who wrote and starred in tremendously popular operettas. He was what was called a "matinee idol" of the London stage, adored by hordes of middle-aged ladies who flocked to afternoon performances and swooned over his romantic looks. His enduring claim to fame is that he wrote the World War I song "Keep the Home Fires Burning."

THE EISTEDDFOD

The great cultural event in Wales is the National Eisteddfod. The word originally meant a "sitting" or "session" of the bards, those poets who sang the praises of the various noble households. The first recorded eisteddfod was held at Carmarthen in 1451. The bards gathered there to discuss the formal rules for the writing of poetry and the poet Dafydd ab Edmwnd decreed twenty-four meters for composition of heroic odes. These are still used today in the National Eisteddfod competition for the Bardic Chair. This is an actual oak chair on which is enthroned the poet who, following rules of rhyme, meter, and subjects, produces the best poem. If none of the poems entered is judged to be of sufficient merit, no Chair is awarded. There is also a Crown, presented for the best free meter poem. All the poems are, of course, in Welsh.

The presentation ceremony is most impressive. It is based on ancient Druid tradition, presided over by an Archdruid who is surrounded by robed figures—all poets or other cultural notables. This band of judges is known as the Gorsedd of the Isle of Britain.

In the nineteenth century, the eisteddfod was extended beyond poetry and now includes dancing and music, from choral singing to brass bands to Welsh rock groups. It is held for nine days in August, alternately in north and south Wales, in different towns. It is a splendid festival that draws huge crowds, not to mention television cameras. There are all kinds of Welsh crafts on sale, exhibits of Welsh industries, lots of things to eat, and a big "language" tent where one can get Welsh lessons.

There is also an International Music Eisteddfod held every July in the little town of Llangollen in north Wales. Its motto is *Byd gwyn fydd byd a gano. Gwaraidd fydd ei gerddi fo:*. Or "Blessed is a world that sings. Gentle are its songs." People come from all over the world to sing, folk dance, and play musical instruments. It is a sort of Olympic Games of the musical world, with none of the tension that too often spoils sporting events. Performances take place in a vast marquee set in a beautiful valley. One of the best features of the event is that all competitors from abroad are

*National costumes worn by folk dancers (left) and
a woman demonstrating the weaving of wool (right).*

housed and fed by local people—at no charge—as a gesture of
goodwill, to foster international friendship.

At an eisteddfod you can see women wearing the Welsh
national costume, and "costume" it certainly is, not to be worn in
ordinary life. It is worn for folk dancing or folk singing, displayed
in museums, and featured on postcards for visitors to send home
to prove they have been in a foreign country.

The costume consists of a long full-skirted black dress, worn
with a black-and-white checked apron, a big white collar (such as
Puritan women wore), a white kerchief over the head and, on top
of that, a high-crowned black hat. This could be described as a
stovepipe hat with a wide brim or a witch's hat with the top
flattened out. An alternative version of the costume has a shorter
red skirt, worn with a white blouse, vest, and overskirt, and a
striped or checked scarf instead of the white collar.

Some sports enjoyed by the Welsh are rugby (above), rock
climbing (bottom left), and hiking (bottom right).

Chapter 10

EVERYDAY THINGS

Wales has plenty to offer the sportsperson. There is fishing of all kinds in the lakes and rivers and in the surrounding sea. Hill and mountain climbing, of course, and marvelous walking routes are available all over, plus spelunking. Canoeing and surfing are popular, especially with visitors, and there are many delightful little harbors all around the coast for sailing buffs.

The sport that the Welsh really care about, however, is rugby. (The game is named from the English school, Rugby, scene of the famous book, *Tom Brown's Schooldays*.) It is similar to American football in that players can be tackled and there are huddles— called scrums—but the rules for tackling are different and the players do not wear helmets or padding. They rely more on agility and speed than brawn. In other parts of Great Britain, rugby is not so widely played and the matches do not attract the huge crowds that soccer does. But in Wales, rugby is the game of all the people. Its fans travel miles to see games and are passionately attached to their teams. An international match is as important as a Super Bowl or World Series.

LEEKS, LAMB, AND LAVERBREAD

The leek is a very important vegetable in Wales. In fact, it is a
national symbol. On St. David's Day—the Welsh equivalent of St.
Patrick's Day—people of Welsh extraction all over the world may
wear a cap with a leek pinned to it. The Welsh supporters at an
international rugby match will brandish leeks as they sing their
Welsh hymns.

The origin of this attachment to leeks is rather hazy. Some say
Welsh soldiers took them into battle because they thought they
cured wounds. Some say that, in the sixth century, the heroic
leader Cadwallader and his men, preparing to fight the Saxons,
saw leeks growing nearby and fastened them to their helmets so
they would spot one another easily in the thick of battle.

The Welsh, however, do not just wave leeks around or wear
them. They cook with them a great deal, using them in soups or
stews and in a particularly popular dish, Anglesey Eggs, made
with eggs, cheese, potatoes, and leeks. Because Wales has been
mostly a poor country, many of its best dishes are concocted from
simple ingredients that the Welsh have been able to raise
themselves. Cheese is the basis for many dishes and, for a long
time, it was made not only from cow's milk but from sheep's milk
or a mixture of both. Most people have heard of Welsh Rarebit
(sometimes mistakenly called Welsh Rabbit). This is a cooked
mixture of cheese, milk, egg, and Worcestershire sauce poured
over toast that is much more interesting than plain old toasted
cheese.

The Welsh, having so many sheep, produce excellent lamb that
is served roasted or stewed with the inevitable leek. There is
plentiful trout from the many rivers, and shellfish—shrimp, crab,

A variety of seafood is available to the Welsh.

cockles, and mussels—from the long coastline. Recently, oyster beds have been cultivated, so there is plenty to eat for those who like gourmet food.

There are many special baked goods to be found in Wales. The women had opportunity to develop their baking skills when coal became plentiful. They became expert with open-hearth baking on large, flat bakestones. You can see how they did it in demonstrations at the Welsh Folk Museum in Cardiff. Baking methods may have changed but the recipes are still used.

The most popular of the baked items is *bara brith,* or speckled bread. This is made with flour, yeast, etc., plus mixed raisins and currants that have been soaked overnight in cold tea. That may sound odd to you, but the tea soaking seems to supply the magic touch. Another favorite is Welsh gingerbread that manages to taste of ginger although no ginger is used in baking it. How's that for a magic touch? Then there are little crumbly cakes, known as Welsh cakes, baked on a griddle. These are distantly related to American biscuits but are generously laden with dried fruit and spices and meant to be eaten as a teatime treat.

Welsh ponies

You would undoubtedly enjoy most of the food in Wales just so long as nobody offered you laverbread, which is seaweed eaten as a vegetable. Of course, you might well enjoy this too if nobody told you what you were eating.

ANIMAL LIFE

The Welsh are great horse lovers. What is claimed to be the biggest horse-trading fair in all Europe is held on the last Thursday of every month in Llanbydder in Dyfed. (Dick Francis, the ex-jockey who has written so many mysteries about horse racing, was born in Wales and lived there as a boy.) Horses feature in many legends including the one about a nineteenth-century horse in Derwenias who startled his owner into sobriety by lecturing him on the evil of his drunken ways.

The Welsh pony is part of the fabric of Welsh life, dating back through history and said to be traced to the Arabian horse. For

Pembroke corgi

long years, when Wales had no decent roads, the sure-footed pony was the only transportation over rocky and boggy paths. This sturdy breed can still be seen on the mountains and can be ridden by trekking tourists. Farmers use ponies when they round up cattle and sheep and people still keep ponies for the pleasure of riding them. Ponies worked down the mines for years and occasionally an old pony who has survived from this era can be seen peacefully grazing in the backyard of an old miner who once worked alongside the animal.

The Welsh are also deeply attached to dogs. In the old days, dogs were used not only for various tasks but were faithful companions. They often accompanied their owners to church and special long-handled tongs were kept there for picking up and ejecting dogs who became restless. Dogs are still essential to every farm and abound in the towns, too. There are two breeds of hunting dog, the Welsh springer spaniel and the Welsh terrier. The real celebrity dog, however, is the corgi. It has been around

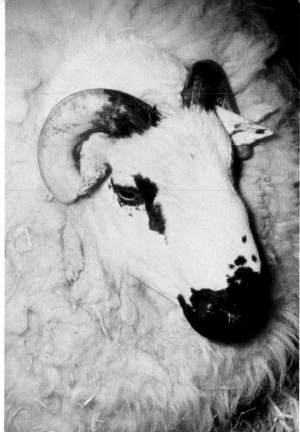

Welsh Black cow with her calf (left) and a Beulah Speckled-Faced sheep (right)

Wales for centuries and has an honorable working record. It has a long, low-slung body and was used by drovers to keep cattle in line by snapping at their ankles. Then in the 1930s, King George VI of England took a corgi into the royal household and, ever since, corgis have been leading a royal dog's life. Naturally, this has made them a very fashionable breed.

Cattle were sacred to the Celts and the white long-horned breed still around today are descended from ancient herds. The Welsh Black, although outnumbered by breeds from England and Europe now, was once the mainstay of the cattle trade and was also used to pull ploughs and wagons. A Welsh Black bull is a particularly fierce-looking beast and one would think twice about approaching him.

A colony of gannets (left) and a puffin (right)

Then the sheep—all those millions—come in various breeds, such as Black Bellied, Badger Faced, and Beulah Speckled-Faced. The Kerry Hill, hailing from Wales, is to be found in America, South Africa, Australia, and New Zealand as well as in its native land. Most pervasive of all is the Welsh Mountain Sheep that can survive in the most forbidding terrain and in the worst of weather.

Birds of all sorts make Wales a bird-watcher's delight. The red kite is the most spectacular among the many species to be seen. Not so long ago almost extinct, it now flourishes. There are buzzards and puffins and the largest colony of gannets in all Europe—more than fifteen thousand of them—is to be found on the little island of Grassholm off the Dyfed coast. Cormorants nest on a huge crag called Bird's Rock, near the Gwynedd coast.

A mixture of Welsh people,
clockwise from above,
includes coalminers,
a farm woman feeding
her lamb, a fisherman,
a child, and a
policeman talking
to a tourist.

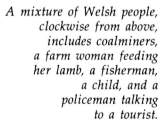

Chapter 11

PARTICULAR PEOPLE

Besides the poets, musicians, and politicians, other Welsh people have made their mark in many ways.

THE GREAT REFORMER

A man of whom the Welsh are very proud is Robert Owen (1771-1858). He was born in Newtown and worked at the flannel looms that operated there when he was a young man. He soon left to set up a cotton-spinning mill in Manchester, in England, and became a very wealthy man. He was also a very enlightened employer and an ardent Socialist. He set up a model town in New Lanark, Scotland, and was a pioneer of the cooperative movement by which workers and consumers receive mutual benefits. (The colony of Welsh in Patagonia was set up in accordance with his theories.) Owen was a prime mover in the Factory Act of 1819, which aimed to reform the abuses of the Industrial Revolution. He established another model community in New Harmony, Indiana in the United States in 1821. The first kindergarten, the first free public school, and the first free public library in the United States were founded here by Owen and his sons. He came home to the

Robert Owen

Bertrand Russell

T.E. Lawrence

place of his birth at the end of his life and is buried there in the churchyard of a medieval church where his elaborate tombstone is a mecca for his many admirers.

AUTHORS

T.E. Lawrence, who became known as "Lawrence of Arabia," was born in Tremadog, Gwynedd, in 1888 and, although he lived there only a year, the Welsh have put up a plaque on the house where he was born. He was famous for his daring deeds with the Arabs during World War I and wrote a magnificent book about his experiences, *The Seven Pillars of Wisdom*.

Bertrand Russell (1872-1970) was born at Trelleck in Gwent. One of the twentieth century's most famous philosophers and a noted figure in intellectual circles for decades, he was an outspoken champion of political and social causes including, in his old age, the "ban the bomb" movement. Among his many books on many subjects, his *The Principles of Mathematics*, published in 1903, is a classic of mathematical logic. His autobiography is well worth reading and his account of his childhood will make you wonder that he survived, let alone grew into a great man. He won the Nobel Prize in literature in 1950. Having lived most of his life in England, he returned to Wales at the age of eighty-three and lived there until his death.

Novelist and playwright Richard Hughes (1900-1976), although not born in Wales, was of Welsh descent and considered himself Welsh. He lived much of his life in Wales and bought a castle at Laugharne where he befriended Dylan Thomas. His most famous book is *A High Wind in Jamaica,* an adventure story about children captured by pirates. It is considered the forerunner of William Golding's *Lord of the Flies*, as it was the first book to treat children in an unsentimental manner. Hughes also had the distinction of writing the first radio play, broadcast in 1924 by the British Broadcasting Corporation.

Jan Morris, the travel writer, is half Welsh and it is obviously her favorite half as you can tell from her book *The Matter of Wales.* It is a marvelous picture of the country, written in a poetic style of which her Celtic ancestors would be proud.

ACTORS

Welsh is a very poetic language and its beautiful sounds produce beautiful voices. It is no mere accident, therefore, that many fine actors have come from Wales.

The most famous of our time is Richard Burton. He was born into a poor miner's family, the last of twelve children. His family name was Jenkins, but he took the name Burton in honor of a schoolteacher who encouraged his talent and inspired him to work for a place at Oxford University. He soon shone there in the famous OUDS (the Oxford University Dramatic Society), which

has been a starting place for many of Britain's most famous actors, including Sir John Gielgud. Gielgud, incidentally, was one of the first to employ Burton on the professional stage.

Burton became a leading Shakespearean actor, playing many great parts such as Hamlet, Othello, and Henry V. He appeared in some memorable films, including *Becket* and *The Spy Who Came in From the Cold*. He also had a huge success in the Broadway musical *Camelot* where his role as King Arthur must have delighted his Welsh soul.

Burton became enormously rich but never forgot his love for Wales. He returned there constantly and generously shared his wealth with his family. He died in Switzerland in 1984 and was buried in Wales.

An early supporter of Richard Burton's talent was actor and playwright Emlyn Williams who became his lifelong friend. He, too, came from a poor Welsh family and was encouraged by a teacher—a woman this time—to get to Oxford on a scholarship. Here he, also, fell under the spell of the OUDS. Not content

Emlyn Williams   *Ray Milland*

merely to act, he wrote plays as well. The best known, *The Corn is Green*, although not exactly autobiographical, is about a poor young Welsh boy taken under the wing of a schoolteacher who sets him on the road to Oxford. The play, in which Emlyn first starred, was made into a movie with Bette Davis as the teacher and later into a TV film with Katherine Hepburn.

Emlyn Williams has written a two-part biography. The first volume, about his boyhood, is called *George*, which is his first name and the name he was called as a boy. The second is *Emlyn*, which is about his stage career. This is his middle name, which he used professionally. *George* is a perfect description of life in Wales and of success through education—a theme dear to Welsh people. Emlyn Williams still appears in films and TV plays.

Ray Milland who became famous in Hollywood, particularly for the film *The Lost Weekend*, was another actor from Wales whose resonant voice was his fortune. Others less well known outside of Britain are Huw Griffiths, Rachel Roberts, and Sian Phillips.

A sculpture of Augustus John (left) and one of his paintings entitled The Blue Pool *(right)*

PAINTERS

It was not till the nineteenth century that any artist could make a living in Wales and the most prominent of these was William Roos (1808-1878). Many of his portraits can be seen in the National Library of Wales collection at Aberystwyth. Later, John Kelt Edwards (1875-1934) and Christopher Williams (1873-1934) were both portraitists who painted, among other important people, Lloyd George.

In the twentieth century, art flourished in Wales and the most famous artist was Augustus John (1878-1961). He was particularly well known for his paintings of gypsies. As a portraitist, he painted such notables as George Bernard Shaw and James Joyce. His portrait of Dylan Thomas hangs in the National Museum in Cardiff. His sister Gwen, although never so famous, was also a painter of great talent.

Another of Wales's most noted painters is Sir Cedric Morris who was one of the first, in the 1930s, to paint the Welsh industrial landscape. Evan Williams (1893-1951) paid tribute to his hometown of Swansea in the paintings he is known for.

Visitors enjoy the countryside and food in Wales.

Favorite artists today include Ferdinand Cirel who is a Cardiff bus driver by trade and Hywel Harris, Brenda Roberts, and Elis Gwyn Jones who are all secondary school art teachers.

INVENTORS AND INNOVATORS

Next time you are working on a math problem and write the equal sign =, you will know that it was Robert Recorde of Tenby who dreamed it up in the 1550s.

In 1861, Sir Pryce Pryce-Jones of Newton started the first mail-order business. Queen Victoria was one of his customers.

Major Walter Wingfield introduced lawn tennis at his residence in Cleyd in 1873.

In 1878, two cousins, Sidney Gilchrist Thomas and Percy Carlyle Gilchrist of Blaenovon, Gwent, perfected the Bessemer process of steel making that revolutionized the steel industry.

Poetic, political, musical, industrious—famous abroad or at home, or just ordinary people—the Welsh, through the centuries, have survived often harsh conditions with their love of their beautiful country and special culture intact. As Jan Morris concludes in *The Matter of Wales*, this is "not just a country on the map, or even in the mind: it is a country of the heart . . ."

MAP KEY

Aberayron	B3	Llandelli	C3
Aberdare	C4	Llandovery	C4
Aberdaron	B3	Llandrindod Wells	B4
Aberdovey	B3	Llandudno	A4
Abergavenny	C4	Llanfyllin	B4
Abertillery	C4	Llangefni	A3
Aberystwyth	B3	Llangollen	B4
Amlwch	A3	Llangynog	B4
Ammanford	C3	Llanidloes	B4
Bala	B4	Llanrwst	A4
Bangor	A3	Lleyn Peninsula	B3
Bardsey Island	B3	Machynlleth	B4
Barmouth	B3	Maesteg	C4
Barry	C4	Menai Strait	A3
Beaumaris	A3	Merthyr Tydfil	C4
Bethesda	A3	Milford Haven	C2
Black Mountains	C4	Mold	A4
Brecon (Brecknock)	C4	Monmouth	C5
Brecon Beacons (mountains)	C4	Montgomery	B4
Bridgend	C4	Narberth	C3
Bristol Channel	C3, C4	Neath	C4
Builth Wells	B4	Nefyn	B3
Burry Port	C3	New Quay	B3
Cader Idris (mountain)	B4	Newcastle Emlyn	B3
Caernarvon	A3	Newport	C5
Caernarvon Bay	A3	Newtown	B4
Caerphilly	C4	Oswestry	B4
Cambrian Mountains	A4, B4, C4	Pembroke	C3
Cardiff	C4	Pontypool	C4
Cardigan	B3	Pontypridd	C4
Cardigan Bay	B3	Port Talbot	C4
Carmarthen	C3	Porthcawl	C4
Carmarthen Bay	C3	Portmadoc	B3
Carmel Head	A3	Prestatyn	A4
Cemaes Head	B3	Presteigne	B4
Chepstow	C5	Pwllheli	B3
Colwyn Bay	A4	Rhondda	C4
Conway	A4	Rhyl	A4
Cwmbran	C4	Rhymney	C4
Denbigh	A4	Ruthin	A4
Dolgellau	B4	Saint Brides Bay	C2
Ebbw Vale	C4	St. David's	C2
Ffestiniog	B4	Saint David's Head	C2
Fishguard	C3	St. George's Channel	B2, C1, C2
Flint	A4	Saint Govan's Head	C2
Gelligaer	C4	Snowdon (mountain)	A3
Glamorgan	C4	Snowdonia	A3
Harlech	B3	Strumble Head	B2
Haverfordwest	C3	Swansea	C4
Hay-on-Wye	B4	Swansea Bay	C4
Holy Island	A3	Tenby	C3
Holyhead	A3	Tregaron	B4
Irish Sea	A3, A4	Tremadoc Bay	B3
Kidwelly	C3	Tywyn	B3
Knighton	B4	Welshpool	B4
Lampeter	B3	Worms Head	C3
Llandeilo	C4	Wrexham	A5

MINI-FACTS AT A GLANCE

GENERAL INFORMATION

Official Name: The Principality of Wales

Capital: Cardiff

Official Languages: English and Welsh. About one-fourth of the people speak Welsh. In some rural areas, about three-fourths speak it. Some newspapers are printed partly or entirely in Welsh, and radio and television programs are broadcast in both languages. Welsh is a form of the ancient Celtic language.

Government: Wales is a part of Great Britain, a constitutional monarchy. Queen Elizabeth II is Britain's head of state, but a cabinet of government officials called *ministers* actually rules Great Britain. The prime minister is the head of government. Wales elects 36 of the 635 members of the British House of Commons.

The chief administrative official is the secretary of state for Wales. The secretary of state heads the Welsh Office in Cardiff. It is responsible for day-to-day administration: housing, local government, national parks, public health, roads, town planning, welfare programs, and water and sewerage systems. The main local units of government are called administrative counties. They in turn are divided into county districts. Wales has eight administrative counties and thirty-seven county districts, each with its own elected council.

A Welsh nationalist party, the *Plaid Cymru*, seeks complete independence from Britain, but most Welsh people are satisfied with their system of government.

Flag: The Welsh flag consists of two horizontal stripes, white and green, with a red dragon superimposed at the center, spouting flames and with a curly tail. The dragon has been a Welsh symbol since the Romans occupied Wales nearly two thousand years ago.

Money: The basic unit is the pound. In October 1986 the British pound was worth $1.43 in United States currency.

Weights and Measures: Wales uses the metric system.

Population: 2,790,462 (1981 census); estimated 1986 population: 2,808,000; distribution; 76 percent urban, 24 percent rural

Major cities:

Cardiff. 269,459
Swansea 183,484
Newport 132,901
Bridgend 128,660
(Population figures based on 1981 census)

Religion: Nearly all Welsh are Protestants. The Methodist church is the largest Protestant church in Wales. Other Protestant religions are Anglican, Baptist, Congregational, and Presbyterian. There are about 140,000 Roman Catholics in Wales.

The Church of England was the etablished church in Wales from 1536 to 1914.

GEOGRAPHY

Highest Point: Snowdon, 3,561 ft. (1,085 m) above sea level

Lowest Point: Sea level along the coast

Coastline: 614 mi. (988 km)

Mountains: The Cambrian Mountains cover about two-thirds of the country. They are steep and rugged in the north. In central and southern Wales, the land becomes flat and forms large plateaus and valleys.

Rivers: The Severn and the Wye are the longest rivers in Wales. They both begin near Aberystwyth and flow eastward into England and eventually empty into the Bristol Channel. The River Dee forms part of the boundary between Wales and England.

Climate: Wales has a maritime climate, dominated by Atlantic air masses. It is characterized by considerable variety and unpredicability. Weather has influenced the life of the country. Rainfall is frequent, with an average yearly total of 53 in. (135 cm).

Greatest Distances: North to south—137 mi. (220 km)
East to west—116 mi. (187 km)

Area: 8,018 sq. mi. (20,768 km²)

NATURE

Trees: The oak forests that once covered Wales are now more or less depleted, and low-lying brushes and marshes prevail, but some forests can still be seen in Snowdonia National Park, Gwydir Forest, Coed-y-Brenin, with streams and cascades, and Brecon Beacons National Park.

Animals: The Welsh pony is part of the fabric of Welsh life. Dogs also are deeply loved by the Welsh people. The Welsh springer spaniel and the Welsh terrier, as well as the corgi, are especially popular breeds. Cattle and sheep also are prevalent.

Birds: Wales is a bird-watcher's delight. The red kite is the most spectacular. Buzzards, puffins, cormorants, and gannets are plentiful.

EVERYDAY LIFE

Food: Roast lamb, roast beef, and mutton stew are favorites. Welsh rabbit (or rarebit) is the most famous dish. It is made of melted cheese and butter, mixed with beer and served on toast, or cheese, milk, egg, and worcestershire sauce. Salmon from Welsh rivers and *bara laver*, a vegetable dish made from seaweed, are popular foods on the Welsh table.

The most important vegetable in Wales is the leek, which in fact has become a national symbol. Leeks are used in soups, stews, and a particularly popular dish called Anglesey Eggs.

Housing: Housing in rural areas is largely made of isolated, whitewashed stone cottages and farm buildings. In the coal-mining regions most people live crowded together in row houses of drab design.

Holidays:

> January 1, New Year's Day
> March 1, St. David's Day, the national saint's day
> Good Friday
> Easter Monday
> Spring Bank Holiday, last Monday in May or first Monday in June
> Summer Bank Holiday, last Monday in August or first Monday in September
> December 25, Christmas Day
> December 26, Boxing Day

Culture: The people of Wales are poets and singers. Welsh literature and music go back to the bards (poet-singers) of the Middle Ages. One of the greatest of the Welsh poems is the *Gododdin*, written about 600, which describes a battle in Yorkshire. Some time before 1147, Geoffrey of Monmouth wrote poems celebrating the legends of King Arthur.

The Welsh legends of the thirteenth and fourteenth centuries are found in *Mabinogion*, a collection of stories based on Celtic myths. Dylan Thomas is the most famous poet of the twentieth century.

A number of cultural institutions foster the development and perpetuation of the arts in Wales: The Welsh Arts Council, the Welsh National Opera Company, the Welsh Theater Company, the National Library of Wales, and the National Museum of Wales.

Sports and Recreation: Rugby is one of the most popular sports in Wales. Football, or soccer, is a favorite on both an amateur and a professional level. Cricket and dog racing are popular in southern Wales.

In the north many people hunt foxes and rabbits. The mountains in Snowdonia National Park in northwestern Wales have excellent climbing areas. Pony trekking, angling and fishing, beaches and bathing, golf, mountaineering and rock climbing, hang gliding, and canal cruising are other activities with wide appeal.

The Welsh love movie-going and participation in all kinds of musical performance.

Communication: There are one morning and two evening newspapers in Wales and many periodicals are published. Welsh BBC and Harlech TV, a commercial company, provide television programs of high quality.

Transportation: Cross-country links in Wales are poor; there is no internally integrated system of transportation. Roads link southern Wales with the English Midlands and southern Wales with London and Bristol.

Railroads go in a similar east-west pattern. Many of the branch lines built in the fifties and sixties are no longer in use. The future of a north-south link is uncertain. There are many picturesque narrow-gauge railroads, however.

There is no direct intercontinental air service to Wales. From Cardiff there are a variety of seasonal flights to English centers as well as to Dublin, Holland, France, Scotland, and the Channel Islands.

Schools: Wales and England have the same school system. Children between the ages of five and sixteen must attend school. There are three types of schools children can attend after they are eleven years old and have taken their *11-plus* examinations. They are grammar schools, which prepare students for college entrance; secondary-modern schools, which provide a general education; and technical schools, which offer vocational training. The University of Wales has colleges in Aberystwyth, Bangor, Cardiff, and Swansea. The University of Wales includes the Welsh School of Medicine and the Institute of Science and Technology at Cardiff and St. David's College in Lampeter.

The adult-education movement flourishes in Wales and offers courses to more adults than does any such system elsewhere in Great Britain.

Health: Health care in Wales is administered through the National Health Service for England and Wales, which has provided comprehensive, free medical care since 1948.

ECONOMY AND INDUSTRY

Agriculture: barley, hay, oats, turnips, potatoes, sheep, cattle
Manufacturing: aluminum, chemicals, electrical equipment, iron, motor-vehicle parts, steel, synthetic fibers, tin plate
Mining: coal, limestone, slate

IMPORTANT DATES

1500-500 B.C. — Bronze Age

1200-600 B.C. — Celts settle in Wales

A.D. 47-80 — Roman armies conquer Wales

51 — Caradog (Caractacus to the Romans) is captured and sent to Rome

1071 — William the Conqueror declares himself lord of Wales

1136 — *Historia Regum Brittaniae (History of the Kings of Britain)* is written by Geoffrey of Monmouth

1170 — Welsh prince, Madog ab Owain, sets forth to discover America

1202 — Llywelyn ab Iorwerth brings most of Wales under his control

1267 — Llywelyn declared Prince of Wales by the English king, Henry III

1282 — English troops kill Llewelyn ap Gruffydd, Prince of Wales, in battle, crushing a Welsh revolt

1301 — Edward I gives the title Prince of Wales to his son

1346 — Several thousand Welsh soldiers leave to fight with the English army in France

1402-10 — Owain Glyndwr revolts against English rule

1451 — First recorded eisteddfod is held at Carmarthen

1457 — Henry Tudor, a Welsh prince, is born in Pembroke

1485 — Henry Tudor becomes King Henry VII of England

1536 — Henry VIII unites Wales and England

1567 — New Testament is translated into Welsh

1588 — Old Testament is translated into Welsh

1644 — Roundheads, under Cromwell, invade Wales

1700s — Methodism takes hold in Wales

1807—Railway line is established between Swansea and the Mumbles

1870—Education Act brings better schools to Wales

1872—University College is founded at Aberystwyth

1880—Compulsory education introduced

1893—University College becomes the University of Wales

1898—South Wales Miners Federation is formed

1900—Keir Hardie is elected to Parliament as the first Labour M.P. by a Welsh coal-mining constituency

1907—Creation of Welsh Department of Education admits the study of the Welsh language in the schools

1911—Foundation of the National Library of Wales is laid

1927—National Museum of Wales opens

1986—Last coal mine, in Rhondda Valley, closes

IMPORTANT PEOPLE

Shirley Bassey, pop singer

Aneurin Bevan (1897-1960), Labour member of Parliament, 1929-1960; Minister of Health, 1945-1951; launched British National Health Service

Sir Frank Brangwyn (1867-1956), artist and mural decorator; did designs for metalwork, stained glass, and tapestry

Sir Edward Burne-Jones (1833-98), painter and designer; started a business in 1862 with William Morris and D.G. Rossetti

Richard Burton (1925-84), Shakespearean actor, film and stage star

Samuel Butler (1835-1902), author, painter, and musician; *The Way of All Flesh* was his autobiographical novel

Thomas Charles (1755-1814), preacher, founder of Welsh Sunday schools

Dafydd ab Edmwnd (c. 1450-1480), poet

Saint David (c. 520-600), patron saint of Wales

W.H. Davies (1871-1940), poet, but known mainly for his *Autobiography of a Super-Tramp*

A.H. Dodd (1891-   ), historian, author of *Short History of Wales*

John Kelt Edwards (1875-1934), portraitist; did painting of Lloyd George

Osian Ellis, harpist

Gareth Evans, opera star

Geraint Evans (1922-   ), opera star

Dick Francis (1920-   ), ex-jockey and mystery writer

Percy Carlyle Gilchrist (1851-1935), with his cousin, S. G. Thomas, perfected the Bessemer process of steelmaking

Giraldus Cambrensis (c.1146-c.1223), nobleman, churchman, scholar, and historian

Owain Glyndwr (c. 1359-c.1416), led rebellion against Henry IV

Henry VII (1457-1509), Henry Tudor, king of England from 1485 to 1509

George Herbert (1593-1633), metaphysical poet; wrote religious works in Latin and English

Alun Hoddinett (1929-   ), composer

Richard Hughes (1900-76), author of *High Wind in Jamaica*

T. E. Lawrence (of Arabia) (1888-1935), Welsh-born archaeologist, soldier, and writer; famous for *The Seven Pillars of Wisdom*

Alun Lewis (1915-44), poet

Richard Llewellyn (1907-76), author of *How Green Was My Valley*

Llewelyn ap Iorwerth (d.1240), called the Great, Prince of North Wales

Llewelyn ap Gruffydd (d.1282), called the Lost, Prince of Wales; recognized as overlord of Wales by Treaty of Shrewsbury, 1265

David Lloyd George (1863-1945), Liberal member of Parliament, 1890-1945; Prime Minister, 1916-22; Chancellor of the Exchecquer; designed first health program in 1911, created Earl of Dwyfor and Viscount Gwynedd of Dwyfor in 1945

Madog ab Owain, a Welsh prince who set forth to discover America in 1170

William Mathias (1934-   ), composer

Ray Milland (1908-1986), Welsh-born Hollywood actor

William Morgan (c. 1545-1604), priest who translated the Bible into Welsh

Sir Cedris Morris, painter

Jan Morris, half-Welsh author of *The Matter of Wales*

William Morris (1834-96), Welsh-born poet, artist, and designer; founded Society for the Protection of Ancient Buildings

John Nash (1752-1815), Welsh-born architect, possibly born at Cardigan; famous for improvements in London's Regent Street and Regent's Park

Nennius (d. 850), wrote *History of the Britons*

Ivor Novello (1893-1951), actor, composer, and playwright; composer of "Keep the Home Fires Burning"

Robert Owen (1771-1859), social reformer; established model community of New Harmony, Indiana, USA

Wilfred Owen (1893-1918), poet whose works were set to music by Benjamin Britten in "War Requiem"

Margaret Price (1941-   ), opera star

Sir Pryce Pryce-Jones, began first mail-order business

William Roos (1808-78), painter of portraits

Daniel Rowlands (1713-90), preacher

Bertrand Russell (1872-1970), philosopher, mathematician

Dylan Thomas (1914-53), author, poet; famous for "A Child's Christmas in Wales" and *Under Milk Wood*

Sidney Gilchrist Thomas (1850-85), metallurgist and inventor; perfected Bessemer process of steelmaking with his cousin, P.C. Gilchrist

Henry Vaughan (1621?-95), metaphysical poet

Thomas Vaughan (1621-95), metaphysical poet

Vernon Watkins (1906-67), poet

John Wesley (1703-91), religious leader; founder, with his brother Charles, of Methodism

Christopher Williams (1873-1934), portrait artist and printer

Emlyn Williams (1905-87), actor, playwright, author of *The Corn is Green*

Evan Williams (1893-1951), painter of Swansea

Grace Williams (1906-77), composer

INDEX

Page numbers that appear in boldface type indicate illustrations

About the Author

Dorothy B. Sutherland was born in Scotland and educated at Glasgow University. Being Scottish, she undoubtedly has a trace of Celtic in her ancestry, which gives her fellow-feeling for the Welsh.

She has lived in London, Hamburg, New York, and Chicago and has worked in publishing for many years. She was advertising and publicity manager at the University of Chicago Press and then founded her own company, which handles advertising and promotion for various publishers. She has reviewed books and teaches a course in publishing in the University of Chicago Continuing Education Program. She is the author of *Scotland* in the Enchantment of the World series.

She can personally vouch for the warmth of Welsh hospitality.